PRAISE FOR *Principaled*

Leadership matters! Barker, Ferrua, and George masterfully identify the areas where it matters the most: knowing yourself, knowing your people, and knowing your skill sets. The authors share personal stories and relevant examples with refreshing honesty and insight into what it takes to stay the course, to help you reflect on your practices and to remind you that what you do matters!

—Jimmy Casas, leadership coach, educator, author, and speaker

Barker, Ferrua, and George's *Principaled* should be required as the go-to playbook for every education leader seeking to lead effectively. The reader is left with the seeds of effective leadership and a developed purpose, and presented with a comprehensive game plan on how effective principals can be cultivated through strategic reflection rather than born out of theory.

—Dr. A. Katrise Perera, 2015 NASS Superintendent of the Year

Being a principal is a rocky ride. Tomorrow always has surprises waiting, there are always too many priorities, and for most of us good is not good enough. It is rare for principals to come out of their schools and share their thinking and their mutual problems, and to help each other smell the roses of success. This is a rare book, written from the front line, and shows the warts and all of becoming and surviving being a school leader. [This book is] chock full of great ideas: fail forward; attend to the controllables; do the right, not necessarily the easy; prioritize that which most impacts student achievement; and embrace hard conversations. It's writing from the heart and soul, and a must-have book for future, new, and experienced school leaders.

—John Hattie, PhD, director of the Melbourne Educational Research Institute

There is no training that can prepare you for the emotional labor required by the role of principal. There are endless courses on building management and instructional leadership, but only the luckiest of us have had great mentors who pass down the real wisdom needed to not only survive in this gig but thrive. In *Principaled*, we find the timeless wisdom necessary to realize the impact we always dreamt we'd have as school leaders.

—Amy Fast, Ed. D., high school principal and author of *It's the Mission, Not the Mandates*

Kate Barker, Kourtney Ferrua, and Rachael George have created a must-have book for school principals, especially those who are new to the role. Combining sound advice, resonant personal vignettes, valuable reflective activities, and just the right amount of research, they have crafted a text that should be required reading in all administrator programs. This book is informative, touching, and witty and promises to be an important addition to the field.

—Angela Peery, Ed. D., consultant, author of *The Data Teams Experience*, *The Co-Teacher's Playbook*, and other titles

Principaled is the book I wish existed when I was a principal. I found myself saying yes constantly and nodding in affirmation throughout each chapter. Being a principal is hard, it's complex, it's demanding, and it's also very rewarding, and learning from three who have such vast experience is invaluable. I loved reading this book, and I know you will, too!

—Adam Welcome, speaker, author, and educator

The principalship offers the highest of highs and the lowest of lows. Kate, Kourtney, and Rachael offer an inside look at the navigation, strategic planning, and realities that principals must understand to be successful in the role. You will find yourself finishing this book with not only fresh ideas for your campus, but a greater understanding of the leadership and service that you can offer your students, staff, and families.

—Adam Dovico, former principal and author of *When Kids Lead*, *The Limitless School*, and *Inside the Trenches*

In this book you will find three experienced principals [who offer] three different perspectives on issues like networking, feedback (receiving and giving), having those hard conversations, and focusing your work on central priorities for you and your staff. *Principaled* is both wonderfully engaging and profoundly insightful.

—Polly Patrick, senior instruction and leadership coach at the International Center for Leadership in Education and author of *Ask, Don't Tell: Powerful Questioning in the Classroom*

Principaled is an immensely readable and informative guidebook written specifically *for* new school administrators *by* experienced principals. The three co-authors authentically share their candid, personal experiences in navigating what it takes to succeed in a role that is often a lonely one due to the immense responsibilities it places on those individuals who assume it. Conveying sincerity, empathy, humor, encouragement, and practical wisdom in a conversational format, this book will be a great resource for *all* school leaders whose inspired purpose is to do the very best they can to create a nurturing, safe, and thriving school environment for the students and teachers in their care.

—Larry Ainsworth, author of *Rigorous Curriculum Design*, *Prioritizing the Common Core*, and *Common Formative Assessments 2.0*

Being a principal is one of the most difficult jobs I've ever had, and yet it's also one of the most rewarding. Baker, Ferrua, and George give heartfelt, experience-laden support in their new book. The personal stories they share will resonate with every administrator. This book is filled with care and love, providing hope for all educators.

—Kyra Donovan, associate partner at the International Center for Leadership in Education, author of *Rigorous Curriculum Design, 2nd Edition*

Leadership can be lonely. Learning the ropes when you are new to leadership or in a new position can be a challenge if you don't have the right resources readily available. *Principaled* is one of those resources that will help you learn how to lead while elevating essential daily practices. Be ready to have this as a resource close by during the course of your career.

—Jessica Cabeen, 2017 Minnesota Nationally Distinguished Principal, author, speaker, and middle school principal

Principaled weaves together powerful insights from three principals with candor, authenticity, care, and humor with invitations to reflect and dig deeper. Whether you're new to your principalship or have been serving as a principal for years, this book will come alongside you with honesty, care, support, and guidance as you navigate your leadership journey.

—Kendra Coates Ed.D., author of *The Girl's Guide to a Growth Mindset* and *Counting What Counts: Reframing Education Outcomes*

Kate, Kourtney, and Rachael's common-sense approach will help you be the best leader you can be. The practices shared here are well worth your time, as a veteran administrator or someone brand-new to a leadership role.

—Amber Teamann, speaker and author of *Lead with Appreciation*

Kate, Rachael, and Kourtney are amazing human beings and truly outstanding leaders. Reading *Principaled* makes you feel like you are in the midst of an incredibly meaningful conversation with your most trusted mentors. Kate, Rachael, and Kourtney generously share their stories, their experiences, and their advice, and in doing so, they provide a treasure trove of invaluable tips and tools for every practicing or aspiring principal.

—Craig Hawkins, executive director of Coalition of Oregon School Administrators

Getting the job is one thing, but being amazing in the job is something totally different and special. Kate, Kourtney, and Rachael crushed it with this sweet mix of practical solutions, real stories, and inspiration! *Principaled* gives us that spark we all need to maximize our personalities and leadership potential for our schools!

—Dr. Andy Jacks, award-winning principal, speaker, author, and NAESP senior fellow

PRINCIPALED

PRINCIPAL*ed*

Navigating the Leadership Learning Curve

KATE BARKER, KOURTNEY FERRUA, AND RACHAEL GEORGE

Principaled: Navigating the Leadership Learning Curve
© 2020 Kate Barker, Kourtney Ferrua, and Rachael George

This book is available at special discounts when purchased in quantity for educational purposes or as premiums, promotions, or fundraisers. For inquiries and details, contact the publisher at books@daveburgessconsulting.com.

Published by Dave Burgess Consulting, Inc.

San Diego, CA

DaveBurgessConsulting.com

Library of Congress Control Number: 2020942917

Paperback ISBN: 978-1-951600-46-4

Ebook ISBN: 978-1-951600-47-1

Cover and interior design by Liz Schreiter

Editing and production by Reading List Editorial: readinglisteditorial.com

To the loves of my life, Rob, Molly, and Andrew, for their never-ending support. For my parents, Bill, Maureen, and Connie, for teaching me the power of love, service, integrity, and hard work.

—Kate

To my sweet family, Kevin, Eva, and Dylan, I love you deeply. For the crew of strong women who amplify and encourage each other, you are the best. For my mom, the strongest woman I know, I am so grateful.

—Kourtney

To one of my greatest mentors and supporters, my husband and fellow administrator, John George.

—Rachael

CONTENTS

INTRODUCTION. 1

PART ONE: REFLECT

CHAPTER ONE: REFLECTION AND REFINEMENT 7
CHAPTER TWO: FIND YOUR PEOPLE AND THE POWER
OF MENTORS 20
CHAPTER THREE: RECEIVE FEEDBACK WITH STYLE 31

PART TWO: FOCUS

CHAPTER FOUR: CLARIFY YOUR PURPOSE 44
CHAPTER FIVE: DECIDE TO GO DEEP 56
CHAPTER SIX: WORK THROUGH YOUR STRENGTHS 75

PART THREE: CONNECT

CHAPTER SEVEN: KNOW YOUR PEOPLE AND NAVIGATE
PERSONALITIES. 90
CHAPTER EIGHT: EMBRACE HARD CONVERSATIONS 105
CHAPTER NINE: DEVELOP YOUR NETWORK. 129
CHAPTER TEN: COMMIT TO YOUR LEARNING 146

PART FOUR: CARE

CHAPTER ELEVEN: FIND YOUR BALANCE 160
CHAPTER TWELVE: SHOW GRATITUDE AND GRACE 177
CONCLUSION: LEAD WITH LOVE 189

RECOMMENDED RESOURCES 205
REFERENCES. 208
ACKNOWLEDGMENTS. 211
ABOUT THE AUTHORS. 212
MORE FROM DAVE BURGESS CONSULTING, INC. 217

INTRODUCTION

"These things will be hard to do, but you can do hard things."

—Glennon Doyle

*W*hether you're brand-new to school leadership, or you've been in your role for a decade, you've probably heard the phrase "leadership matters." We believe that it matters immensely, and as school administrators, we strive to make good on that statement. But if you want to get good—or get even better—at this gig, you've probably come face-to-face with some tough truths: Being a principal is hard; being a principal is lonely; being a principal absolutely sucks sometimes. The unpredictable nature of this job means that your role on any given day could range from navigating a parent dispute, delivering news about a position being cut, putting the school on lockdown, or navigating school closures amid a pandemic. Some of you will work on a team of administrators, while others stand alone in the office.

All too often, administrators are expected to know the answers, remain incredibly positive, and never show weakness in a field of desolate isolation. The learning curve can feel unsurmountable and incredibly isolating. Educational leaders are expected to be the calm in the storm, whether they are changing outcomes with student achievement, navigating a parent who is angry, or leading while our nation, districts, and neighborhoods wage battle about reopening school in the middle of a pandemic.

The truth is that this work is human work, and in order to be good at it, you have to connect to your own humanity in a very real, authentic way. This means finding a way to lead through your own strengths and personality, to connect and deliver the work in a way that is uniquely you, while also weaving in the collective wisdom from research and experience to help you bring your school to its fullest potential. It's hard to do all of these things well by yourself. We believe that principals need and deserve a posse of other administrators to champion and amplify them. This is where we want to step in and offer our support. You are not alone. We believe you can do it, and we can help.

This book is about amplification. The work that principals do is critically significant, and staying the course, learning as you lead, and becoming better at what you do gets a lot easier when you're able to do it with the support of colleagues, mentors, and a community. This work is too challenging to embark on alone. As three principals with, collectively, over thirty-five years in the principalship, we're here to help you remember that you're not in this by yourself. We'll share the lessons we've learned on the road, the scars we've come to sport, and the mountains we've climbed. Five of the big pillars we've established to ground our practice are reflection, focus, connection, care, and love.

If you feel like you're still at the steep part of the learning curve, we're each extending a hand to help pull you up to where you can find your footing. If we have done our job well, by the time you finish this book, we will have laughed together, cried together, grown together, and explored some tangible methods for building your own skills as an instructional leader and culture-creating royalty. We believe that every principal who is willing to put in the work can achieve incredible outcomes for kids. We want to be on your team and help you do it.

HOW THIS BOOK CAME TO BE

Oh my goodness, these are my people, and I desperately need them in my life! A few years ago, the three of us felt just this way when we met at a principals' conference hosted by our state's administrator organization. Although we were from very different school districts spanning Oregon and were at various stages of life, we felt an immediate connection and a sense of sisterhood. The fact that we happen to resemble each other was a humorous bonus, and we've long joked, with a nod to Madonna, about going on a Blond Ambition tour of our own.

We knew we had something special from the beginning. We were all incredibly dedicated principals who were constantly striving to improve our student achievement, bolster a positive school climate, and, in the midst of our work, find some sense of balance in our lives. We were data-driven, research-rich administrators who wanted to find a way to implement best practices and turn big ideas and dreams into realistic accomplishments. We were also brutally and refreshingly honest about our faults, missteps, and opportunities for growth. As our trust and respect for each other grew, we spent hours sharing ideas and problem-solving situations. These days, we're each other's champions as much as we are collaborators. We pick each other up on defeating days and are the first to celebrate each other's triumphs.

At a conference not long ago, we were having dinner with Jessica Cabeen, a national keynote speaker. She leaned across the table and said to us, "Do you know how unique this is?" We remember looking at Jessica puzzled. She was alluding to the synergy between the three of us and the absence of a bitter competitive edge. Instead, she noticed, we seemed to genuinely take pride in and cheer on each other's work. It's true! We are invested in our relationship with one another, because it makes our own work stronger. What's more, we hope others will adopt this kind of collaborative model by building their own professional networks and leveraging leadership in a way that promotes strong school culture and student success.

WHO WE ARE

Kate Barker

As a teacher, mentor, and principal, Kate Barker believes that everything starts with a genuine relationship. Connections and high expectations are at the core of her philosophy. After thirty years of dedicating her career to a diverse group of students, staff, and families, Kate still loves teaching students and adults, creating beautiful bulletin boards, and opening up a new box of crayons. Her greatest growth and joy has come from learning from fellow educators, community partners, students, and families. Decades later, she still thinks she has the best profession in all the world, and she looks forward to sharing practical strategies, epic fails, and real stories with you.

Kourtney Ferrua

After ten years in the classroom, Kourtney became an elementary principal in the same district where she had been an instructional coach and kindergarten teacher. She found the principalship to be a lot like motherhood, where you think you know a lot about it until you actually go through it. Luckily, she surrounded herself with wise mentors, trusting colleagues, and a staff who never gave up. In a short amount of time, through collaborative leadership and a focus on teaching and learning, things improved immensely. In 2019, Kourtney was recognized as Oregon's Elementary Principal of the Year and a National Distinguished Principal. Kourtney's "why" is deeply seated in the replication of success, and she loves helping administrators amplify their impact on kids.

Rachael George

Rachael loves to work hard and play hard, and her approach can be observed in how she tackles each day. She is an early riser and loves to fill the hours with challenges and opportunities for growth and learning. While she has taught in and led buildings at both the secondary and elementary level, she has most recently settled at the elementary level, where she is living the dream and helping students grow. She is deeply involved with the Coalition of Oregon School Administrators and actively engaged in work with the National Association of Elementary School Principals (NAESP). Rachael loves her job and can't think of anything she would rather do.

— PART ONE —

REFLECT

CHAPTER ONE

REFLECTION AND REFINEMENT

"Picture your brain forming new connections as you
meet the challenge and learn. Keep on going."

—Carol Dweck

We know what you're thinking: Reflect? What principal has time to stop and reflect? Your first year as an administrator can feel like driving ninety miles an hour with your head out the window and your eyes closed. Hey, it can feel that way for years. Many principals spend their first weeks in their new role with their heads spinning, looking around and saying, "Oh! That's my job? That's my job, too? Oh! That's also my job." No matter what steps you take to prepare, it's normal to feel overwhelmed by the scope, pace, and all-encompassing nature of the gig. And in your first year, you'll probably experience some failure, make a few mistakes, and feel completely overwhelmed. It's the part of the work that no one ever talks about, and it can feel particularly disheartening to the many of us who are drawn into leadership because we want to replicate past successes on a bigger scale. We tend to be ambitious, driven, goal-oriented, and, yes, perhaps just a little bit confident.

It is common to experience failure or missteps that might take your breath away. It's okay. It's normal. The key to success is not to avoid failure, but to *fail forward*. We can do this by reflecting, taking ownership, and learning strategically from when things go wrong. When you get into the habit of going through this process, you'll have the opportunity to leverage growth in incredible ways.

So, back to that time you think you can't make for reflection. Maybe you've convinced yourself that if you just keep going, maybe faster and more furiously, whatever it is that's not going great will fix itself, and things will turn around. But can you think of a time when that worked for you? The risk of going full throttle in the wrong direction is that you'll find yourself exhausted, defeated, and further from the work that will make a difference for students. Our advice: STOP. Not forever, but long enough to reflect with *purpose*.

Kourtney

In my first year as a principal, I worked harder and longer than I ever had, but it seemed like everywhere I turned I was reminded of how much I sucked at it. I was living in triage, stressed beyond belief, and never took time to breathe let alone reflect.

That October, I was sitting alone in my office at 7:00 p.m., staring blankly at my computer, when my superintendent called with a cryptic message: "Meet me at the restaurant at the corner in five." When I walked in, she was sitting at a table with the director of human resources. *Well this was the shortest career in history!* I thought. She told me to have a seat and order something. Food was about the last thing I wanted. My stomach was in my throat, and it was all I could do not to bust out into the ugly cry.

"Something came to my attention at the union meeting tonight that I want to talk to you about," she said. "I hear that you moved some mailboxes."

WHAT?! She called me over here to meet her for this?

"I alphabetized them," I responded.

"Some people have had those mailboxes for twenty years," she said. I nodded blankly. "What did you learn?" she prompted.

"They care a lot about mailboxes," I said slowly.

"I think you will find that they care deeply about a lot of things, and that's not a bad thing," she mentored. With pointed questions and gentle prompting, she helped me to realize that I was missing a big part about leadership: reflecting on how I was received by others.

The next day, I called an optional meeting in one of the classrooms, and we sat in a big circle. Since I'd started, I had been so hesitant to be vulnerable or demonstrate any sign of weakness; but at this meeting, I showed my cards. I took a deep breath and said, "Guys, this isn't going well, and I need your help to fix it. I feel like I've made mistakes that I didn't know were mistakes. I want to give us space to talk about it, and I need your ideas about how we can fix it." The air in the room shifted; people started talking and things started moving in a positive direction. Sometimes the most beautiful outcomes grow out of the worst experiences.

Start by identifying what is working well with your personal leadership toolkit and in your school-wide systems. Think about the parts of the job that come naturally and feel effortless. The beauty of this question is that the answers will be different for all of us who embark on such important work. You do this job by bringing your own qualities to the work. Perhaps you are excellent at building relationships with families, or you were just the right person to spark new energy among the staff. Maybe you're the king of problem-solving and a whiz at master schedules, or maybe your skill is in getting the traffic line moving like a breeze.

Go through the 752 hats you wear on a daily basis and make a long list of the things that you are doing well. If the list doesn't come easily, think harder, or ask a trusted colleague to help you brainstorm. The truth is, you're always doing more things right than wrong. Your unique skills, experience, and perspective are why your school hired you to do this job in the first place. It may not be as easy to see these positive attributes, especially when you are feeling defeated. Spend a little time with your successes and allow yourself some grace. You are working hard, and these triumphs deserve recognition, gratitude, and admiration.

WHAT'S NOT WORKING? WHAT MAKES YOU MAD? WHERE ARE YOUR OBSTACLES?

Next, write down everything that's frustrating you. Be brutally honest. Let it all out. Get everything that stinks down on paper right now. Feel whatever emotion this evokes and write with reckless abandon. (Names are okay! After all, this list is for your eyes only.)

When you have your (likely long) list of everything that feels like an obstacle between you and success, step back for a minute, breathe, and just feel. Whatever you feel is all right. Write down what each of your frustrations evokes. Intense emotion indicates that you care deeply for the work you do and urgently want to be better at it. You may even be mad because students are still not experiencing success under your watchful eye—and that is a worthwhile thing to be angry about. Sit with however you feel. Wallow, even. You have exactly ten minutes for your pity party, and then it's time to get to work.

Take a moment and write down five frustrations and the emotions they invoke:

Frustration	Invoked Emotion
1.	
2.	
3.	
4.	
5.	

What can you prioritize? How do you know what to focus on first?

Ten minutes up? Great. Now that you've taken some time to sit with your feelings, take another look at those frustrations and sort them into two categories: "things I can control" and "things I cannot control." For example, if the neighbor across the street from the school is leaving you messages about being woken up by the roar of a bus engine going over a speed bump at 8:00 a.m., that is frustrating. But short of cutting off her phone service, there's not much you can do to stop her from complaining. Similarly, if the PTA president is slamming you on Facebook, sure you can engage in a conversation with him, but ultimately you do not control his behavior. You also don't control other people's attitudes, actions, or thoughts. Trying to do so will smother your joy like quicksand, swallow you up, and make you lose your traction.

Frustration	Things I Can Control	Things I Cannot Control
1.		
2.		
3.		
4.		
5.		

Now take a look at the list of things that you can control. As you sift through them, see if themes start to emerge (i.e., scheduling, safety, relationships, instruction, climate, facilities). Note these themes or categories.

Frustration Identification

Example

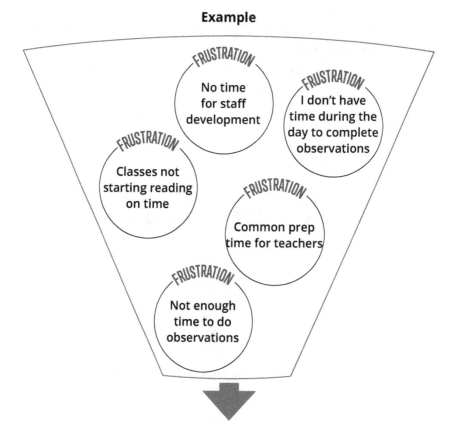

Category: Time

Your Turn

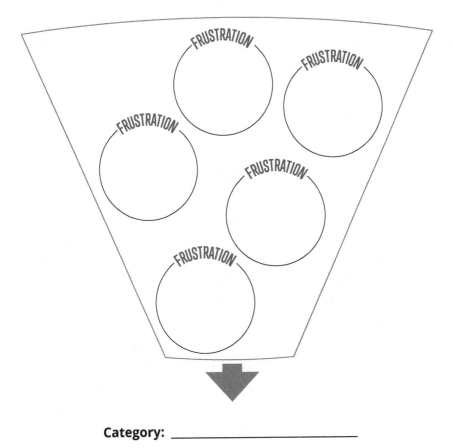

Category: _____

─────────────────── Rachael ───────────────────

I jumped into the principalship in a district that was brand-new to me. My building had a different student population than I was used to, and getting to know the school community was vital. Instead of reflecting on myself as a leader, the staff and I had to reflect on the school as a whole in order to figure out what was working, what wasn't, and how we were going to move forward. That year, I started off this reflection process by visiting with each of my staff members, from the kitchen staff, to the educational assistants, to the teachers, to see what their thoughts were on how things were going. We talked about what they were proud of and about areas where they wanted to see some change. This was very eye-opening, as I found everyone was quick to throw other people under the bus at the first opportunity.

Regardless, it really helped me see what areas I could leave alone for the time being, while working on other areas that were more pressing, based on stakeholder input.

While many of us want to take everything on at once, trying to do so will cause serious burnout—and fast. So, where do you start? In my current building, we as a staff spent my entire first year working to define what we stood for and what we didn't. This involved many long talks about our core values and what we believed to be true for education. We first agreed that our focus would be on growing all kids, regardless of where they came in at, then we talked about how we were going to grow our kids. We were able to zero in on three key areas: academics, attitude, and attendance. We believed that if we could target those key areas, we could change the world when it came to growing students.

Once this was all settled on, we faced an even more difficult job as we talked about what we were going to take off the table so we could move these three areas forward. This was a hard, hard conversation, as it involved some topics that were near and dear to the hearts of the teachers, but were not in alignment with the direction we were headed as a staff. For my part, I just facilitated the conversation for the staff while they worked through various pet projects and programs as we aligned our work. By the end of the first year, we had a clear direction of where we were headed and how we were going to get there. Truth be told, there were some staff members who left after that first year.

Prioritizing your themes/categories comes next, and each needs to be ranked based on its impact on student achievement. Read that again: *student achievement.* It's important to remember that our mission lies in teaching and learning. In this day and age, that message can get muddied. Some experts may tell you to first address culture and climate and worry about student achievement down the road, but we know better.

You must do both. This will be your students' only year in a particular grade. If you choose to forego academic achievement to develop culture, behavior, or social-emotional learning, you are choosing to create achievement gaps. Yes, we said it. The decisions you make will either create more opportunities for kids, or have the potential to create more challenges. That said, there are amazing examples of strong principals across the country who find balance among the various components that leverage student success, including academics, soft skills, culture, social-emotional learning, etc.

You have to be intentional and clear in the initiatives you choose, because here's the thing: you *can* do it all, you just can't do it all at the same time. When you prioritize based on student achievement, you are putting the most important goals first and will have the opportunity to see incredible results. So, choose one indicator and dive deep. If you haven't already, look to research to ground yourself in what the experts in education are pointing to as the high-leverage opportunities for shifting student achievement. Imagine, for example, being frustrated that teachers aren't able to pinpoint where students are in their learning at any given time and are surprised by the results on summative assessments. Every. Single. Time. Exasperating, right?

In his book *Visible Learning for Teachers*, educational researcher John Hattie shows that formative assessment, professional collaboration, and feedback have profound impacts on student achievement. Alleviating this frustration might mean creating alignment for common formative assessments with teacher teams so they can discuss student evidence regularly and identify specific trends in errors and misconceptions. Teacher teams can then plan their feedback loops and goal-setting for individual students.

There is vast agreement in the educational research of Rick DuFour, Rebecca DuFour, Linda Darling-Hammond, Robert Marzano, John Hattie, Douglas Reeves, and Mike Schmoker: as you embark on your prioritization, it is critical that you are well versed in the key elements that will advance student achievement, such as a clear curriculum, formative assessment, professional collaboration, and high-impact teaching strategies. Still, while you might perceive the steps toward school improvement as straightforward, don't confuse "straightforward" for "easy." Remember that, even when it feels like the weight of the world is on your shoulders, you're not alone. (More on that later.)

> Remember that, even when it feels like the weight of the world is on your shoulders, you're not alone.

While student achievement should be your first priority, there may be ways to simultaneously address the culture of your school. Let's say you are frustrated by the staff's low morale, and you feel your team lacks the energy to inspire a different outcome for kids. Spend a bit more time reflecting, and it might become clear to you that the staff is not feeling appreciated or recognized for their hard work. This is very common with new leadership or tired leadership. When we are stressed out and running on the hamster wheel, it is common to forget to pause and appreciate others. It's also common to feel a little bitter about it. (Remember, we are being honest here!) As a new (or seasoned) administrator, you are most likely working harder than you ever have before, and fielding complaints when you already feel like you're going full-throttle can be tough. Simply pause for a bit and do a reset. After all, you cannot change the actions or behaviors of others. The only power move you have is to control your perceptions and to presume positive intentions.

No one on earth wakes up in the morning and asks, "How can I be mediocre and slightly annoying today?" If people are complaining, listen for the underlying concern. Presume that whoever's sharing a complaint has a constructive purpose, and focus on what they are saying rather than the tone or method they are using to say it. Presume they are sharing their frustration (perhaps not in the most productive way) because they want the learning environment to improve. Try to be grateful for the feedback, because, as Maya Angelou said, "When you know better, do better."

In addressing low morale, focus on the positives: identify what is working and spread *authentic* appreciation. (Emphasis on the "authentic" piece. If you don't genuinely feel it, don't say it. People can smell a false compliment a mile away.) Start small, keep it manageable, and let the way you express your gratitude reflect your style. A hand-written note after a walkthrough can do wonders, and may hang on a teacher's bulletin board by her desk for months afterward. Taking the time to recognize a specific act in person can turn someone's gloomy day into a bright one. Giving kudos in your weekly or daily bulletin can make the recipient swell with pride. An email shout-out or a classroom announcement can make for sunnier attitudes. You might think that a morale boost requires a Pinterest-worthy staff room makeover, a coffee cart every Friday, or delivering cute treats in every color of the rainbow to classrooms. This might be your thing, but it may not be. Either way is okay. The essential thing is that your appreciation of others needs to align with your style so that it can be received as authentic and genuine.

Kate

I like to think of appreciation as a form of compensation. Saying thank you or completing an act of kindness to show gratitude is second only to sending out paychecks at the end of the month. I truly believe that leaders can move mountains by showing their appreciation to their network of staff, colleagues, and the greater community. Appreciation is the universal language of "I see you, and I value what you are doing."

To appreciate, you need to differentiate. Getting to know the members of your staff and recognizing how they like to *receive* appreciation is critical. As many of us have learned from Gary Chapman's *The 5 Love Languages*, we typically show our love and appreciation in the same way we like to receive it. (If you haven't checked out this book, do!) Be mindful. I used to universally praise my staff at meetings and assemblies, assuming they liked to be publicly recognized and fawned over in front of peers. Finally, a brave soul shared that this kind of recognition caused them to cringe, turn red, and slink under the table. Oops!

Everyone's different. I have teachers who have saved handwritten cards, yellowed and brittle, on the insides of their closets for years.

Other notes, I see tossed into the recycling bin at the end of the class period. Some staff members love to receive Starbucks cards, while others just want twenty minutes of your undivided attention and to hear you say, "I see what you have done and appreciate your hard work." One of my favorite acts of appreciation is to write a letter of gratitude to my teachers' parents. My assumption is: What mom or dad doesn't like to hear that their son's or daughter's boss thinks they are meaningfully contributing to shaping children's lives?

Get to know which of your staff prefer hugs, handshakes, and fist bumps, and which prefer to have their personal space preserved. Anyone who knows me knows that I am a hugger. However, I have several staff members who like a little less human contact. I'll never forget one of my first days as a principal in my current building. A staff member who knew me well was introducing me to a teacher I had never met before. He said in that very first moment, "Kate, this is Kathy. She doesn't hug." While he was smiling at the time, it was a warning. I appreciated his candor. He saved both Kathy and me from uncomfortable moments.

The point is, one size doesn't fit all. As you spend time getting to know your staff and their gratitude style, invite them to share with you, via letter, email, or survey, how they like to receive praise and appreciation. This way, staff members have an avenue to proactively share with you, instead of mustering up the courage to tell you in person or at an inopportune moment. Regardless of how you go about it, showing appreciation is one of the best ways to build nurturing and positive relationships. It makes the other person feel great, and it will make you feel spectacular, too.

Whatever your priorities, by the end of this first phase of reflection, you should have an action plan for one or two goals to improve your school. Bring your priorities to your site council or teacher advisory group. Structure feedback in a way that helps give you insight into others' perceptions, but not in a way that could derail the improvement. You want feedback to enhance the plan, so think carefully about how you will frame that conversation. It is important to begin with your own reflection, including the educational research and prioritization process, before bringing your plan to your leadership team. Equip your team with the information they'll need to give you efficient and effective criticism, so they don't get off track and focus on the wrong priorities.

Remember, *you can do it all*, just not at the same exact moment. Go deep with a few goals. Trying to tackle too many at once may lead to shallow and ultimately ineffective outcomes. With a sense of focus, you'll be able to discern if issues that arise fit into your current vision for improvement or need to be addressed at a later point.

Taking time to be reflective and dream about the possibilities may at first seem like one more task to add to your to-do list, but it's critical. Through frequent reflection, you are setting an example as the lead learner in your building. This is important not just to affirm your current actions, but to look with a critical eye at what improvements you could make for students. Leaders who are reflective embrace new understandings while folding research and best practices into their work. These folks are our favorite because they live in the realm of possibilities and foster a mission of equitable outcomes for all students.

INVITATION TO IMPLEMENT

Productive reflection requires intentionality, consistency, and the right conditions—so make a plan.

- What kind of environment (office, coffee shop, home, bar) do you need to do your best reflecting?
- For the next month, schedule thirty minutes per week to think deeply about your practice.
- Take some time to fill out the graphic organizers in this book.
- What data points do you need to plan for success at your school?
- How might you combine personal reflection and data review to get your finger on the pulse of your building?

CHAPTER TWO

FIND YOUR PEOPLE AND THE POWER OF MENTORS

"Colleagues are a wonderful thing–but mentors, that's where the real work gets done."

–Junot Diaz

*I*magine you have been asked to give a speech for a community event with an audience you want desperately to impress. After pouring over every word for weeks, you decide to run your speech by a handful of your favorite colleagues. When you finish the final sentence, with your eyes wide open and waiting for their thoughts, Friend Number One says, "Brilliant!" Friend Number Two says, "You are going to do great!" Friend Number Three twists her lips and says gently, "It doesn't sound like you. You are trying to be too formal, and it comes off cold and distant. I want to hear YOU. Your passion comes out so well when you tell stories about your staff and students, but you didn't mention them at all."

Ouch. Talk about the honest truth. Back to the computer you go. And while your confidence might be smarting a bit, you also manage to write from the heart a speech that inspires others and reflects your vision. Thanks, Friend Number Three.

Mentors are critical to the evolving leader, and they come in different forms. While it is important to have colleagues in your circle who can pump you up, give you energy, and support you unconditionally, it is equally important to have a Friend Number Three in your professional arsenal. This is the person who's able to give you the transparent feedback necessary to know what to move forward with and what to put back on the rack.

Leadership roles in schools are often solitary, and can be incredibly lonely and virtually impossible to do effectively without support and feedback. Mentors are there when you are drowning and need a helping hand to reach the surface. They are there to celebrate accomplishments and carry you on your darkest days. Mentors listen intently, hand over tissues, and know when a happy hour is needed.

We all gravitate toward people who are most like ourselves. We typically hire people who are most like ourselves. We sit by people in meetings who are most like ourselves. And we tend to seek feedback from people who are—you guessed it—most like ourselves. While these people *are* great for collaborating and brainstorming over coffee, you may be limiting your opportunity for feedback by staying in your comfort zone. Pause for a moment and recognize the limitations in surrounding yourself with people who are like yourself. Think about the ways that narrow focus limits how you make decisions, what you value, and what you see in your environment, or don't. We challenge you to find mentors who stretch your thinking, respectfully disagree with you,

> We challenge you to find mentors who stretch your thinking, respectfully disagree with you, and unwrap your security blanket.

and unwrap your security blanket. Think of it as working out. It may hurt during and after, but ultimately it makes you stronger. It does mean your skin will need to develop a few more layers, but guaranteed your blind spots will become fewer and fewer, and your perspective will widen, leading to more inclusive practices.

Kate

One summer, several years ago, I was pondering what to do with my teachers during those precious few days before the students' voices would fill the nooks of our building. Typically, we would do some team bonding, look at data from the previous year, and talk about systems and structures. Although the font would change and the "flavor of the year" initiatives would shift, the agenda stayed largely the same. I owed my incredibly talented staff more. I yearned to do something different, something inspiring, something positive. I intended to do something that would stretch their thinking while building connections. I wanted to honor and capitalize on their strengths, while growing our professional practice together. But how?

I turned to one of my mentors. This particular mentor I've known since I was fourteen. Stacey and I are an unlikely pair who met on the volleyball court. She was the six-foot star player, and I stood almost a foot shorter, destined to fill the role of "athletic supporter." I hit the jackpot in both the best friend and mentor categories with Stacey, now a wickedly smart and creative leader at a top Fortune 500 company. Since she is outside of the educational realm, she brings a fresh perspective to the management of people, systems, and structures.

While discussing my school-year kickoff dilemma with Stacey on a walk one Sunday afternoon, she told me about the work of Gallup executives Tom Rath and Barry Conchie, and their book, *Strengths Based Leadership*. She had recently been through a training with her team and raved about the concept. I was hungry for more details, and she graciously shared her resources. I was hooked!

And so, on those precious few days before the fresh coat of floor wax was scuffed, I took a risk, and my staff and I took a totally new tack that year. We filled out the *Strengths Based Leadership* survey, identified our strengths, and discovered together why being so different from one another was an asset, not a deficit. We learned both the positives and drawbacks of our identified strengths. Most importantly, we learned how to make use of our strengths to better complement each other.

When you are stymied about what to do next and looking for fresh ideas, don't be afraid to search beyond your professional realm of influence and capitalize on someone else's know-how.

The great thing about mentors is that you get to choose them. Consider filling these three roles:

- **Colleague-mentor**: Someone who will help you navigate the system of your district.
- **Professional network mentor**: Someone who will inspire you and help you see the big picture in your field.
- **Ugly cry mentor**: Someone who can see you at your lowest moments, knows all of your secrets, and loves you deeply anyway.

You may win the lottery and find one individual who checks all three of these boxes, but that's not usually the case. The benefit of having different people designated for different roles is that you get multiple perspectives and can weave their feedback together in a way that feels authentic to you. (Side note: Your spouse/partner/friends will thank you for finding other mentors, too. As it turns out, unloading on your loved ones every night can be hard on relationships. Unless your partner is also an administrator [Rachael's is!] chances are they will tire of hearing about your work life.)

A **colleague-mentor** could be a veteran administrator in your district, or someone who has just navigated the first years in their role. As you are considering your selection, think about seeking out someone who has experienced success, or whose "why" for the work is similar to your own. In some districts, you may be given an "official" mentor, perhaps another principal or director in your district. This person may be incredibly useful at helping you understand the nuts and bolts of the position, district culture, and expectations. But be cautious with these partnerships. Sometimes colleague-mentors are not the best confidants. There are a lot of politics at play in leadership positions, and you may not know who is going back and sharing information with others. Until you feel completely comfortable, you may not want to show all of your cards to someone within your system. You just never know how people within communities are connected, and the last thing you want is to be judged by your weakest moment. Keep your conversations with this person to safe topics, and work to build a relationship that will leverage student achievement across the system.

For your **professional network mentor**, consider connecting with another leader in a neighboring district through your state's professional organization. This provides the opportunity to talk about systems outside of your district. There are also great professional learning networks on social media that frequently bring up hot topics and engage in conversation about the work. It's nice to have someone outside of your system so that when you are looking for new ideas for the nuts and bolts, you can get an outside perspective from someone who is still in the field. This type of mentor can also become an innovation partner, sharing new research and ideas that stretch your own thinking and the thinking within the field.

As you consider your **ugly cry mentor**, think instead about someone who's had your back in the past. This could be a college professor or a retired administrator from your first years as a teacher. Reach out and invite them to coffee, think of questions to ask them about their journey in leadership, and invite them to give you advice. The best mentorships will evolve into regular rendezvous with deep dialogue and refreshing insights. You will want to select a person who is known for their confidentiality and wisdom. This is a person who will always answer your texts and will be brutally honest with you. Meeting with this person regularly can help you grow exponentially, but you have to make time in your calendar and space in your heart for it. We suggest scheduling a regular date on the calendar, so you have the time blocked out. Prioritizing your own development is critical to success as a leader. (Hint: Don't cancel your regularly scheduled date because you are too overwhelmed. The time when you feel like you don't have time for your mentor is usually the time you need them most!)

While you are working on identifying possible mentors, a word of caution: don't be the mentee that walks up to someone and literally asks them to be your mentor. This question comes out of left field and it's just plain awkward for the person you are asking. Instead, find someone that is on a similar career path to yours, or who has similar interests in an area you want to develop. Reach out to them and make a genuine connection. Perhaps you can ask for their input on a project you're working on, or for advice on a challenge you're facing. Consider, too, that being a mentor involves someone giving you their time and energy, so think about how you can give back. This needs to be a reciprocal relationship. Perhaps you can volunteer your time to help support a project they are working on, both to return the favor of their attention and also to establish credibility. After all, mentors tend to gravitate toward and support people they believe have potential.

So, who can you reach out to as a potential mentor? Here's your chance to brainstorm. As you list these names, consider where you'll intersect with these individuals and in what context you'll be able to evaluate their potential as a mentor for you. A few suggestions for where to look: at conferences; on social media; on district, regional, or state committees; on boards, in workgroups; or possibly in your yoga class. Don't forget, mentors can also include wise family members or the lifelong friends who may know you the best.

Identifying Mentors

Colleague-mentor
1.
2.
3.
Action: Where might you connect with these mentors?

Professional network mentor:
1.
2.
3.
Action: Where might you connect with these mentors?

Ugly cry mentor:
1.
2.
3.
Action: Where might you connect with these mentors?

Kourtney

Before I was an administrator, I was an instructional coach. What an amazing gig that was! It was all rainbows and unicorns. You walk in and help teachers who have signed up to work with you. They are collaborative and think your ideas are the bee's knees!

By contrast, my first year as an administrator was pretty rough. Already, I was seen as being out of touch with the classroom. I was putting in more hours than ever before, yet nothing was working to shift the paradigm at my school. The armor I had to put on each day started to feel heavier and heavier.

The curriculum director had been my boss when I was an instructional coach. She knew me well, but I was trying so hard to maintain the facade that everything was going great. I was afraid to show any kind of vulnerability. One day when I walked into her office to turn something in, she said softly, "You doing okay, Kourt?" My lips quivered, my eyes filled, my nose started leaking, and a huge softball lodged in my throat. The body-shaking sobs came from a visceral place. She nodded gently, closed her door, and asked her secretary to tell her next meeting she'd be late. Then she held me.

When I came up for air, I felt so ridiculous. Clearly, I was not meant for this work if my skin was so thin. I admitted to her that I didn't know if I could do this. "Oh no," she said, "this is exactly why you should do this work. You're sad because you care." She was right. We need administrators who care deeply and are reflective enough to know when things aren't working. She then did what a good mentor does: she asked me questions. Things like: Does your staff know that you care about them? How are you helping them know why you want to do this work? Are you allowing them to know you as a person? She encouraged me to bring my personality and humanity to the work. "Focus and dig deep," she advised.

The next day, I got up, but did not put on the armor to prepare for my day. I moved a little slower, which felt unnatural at first. I created space for connections and focused on building relationships. And, gradually, things got easier. My mentor knew me well enough to reflect my weakness back to me with love and support. I am forever grateful that she saw me when I needed it most.

Matching with a mentor is a little like dating. It takes time to know if they are the right fit for you. You may have to go on several blind dates before you find the right match. Be patient and don't give up. And just like courting, there needs to be chemistry, shared goals, and a willingness to enter into a relationship. Like any great partnership, mentors and mentees work best when there is a circle of trust and the ability to be brutally honest with the intention of helping each other grow. Also like dating, you have the opportunity to put yourself out there and be proactive about seeking like minds. While this is not as easy as Match.com, it follows the same principles. Go to professional events you feel passionate about. Connect with other administrators on Twitter who share your visions. Ask deep questions of other professionals about how they have inspired change and risen from their stumbles.

> Matching with a mentor is a little like dating. It takes time to know if they are the right fit for you.

Recognize that sometimes the connection is a misfire, and just like dating, it's not necessarily about you. Timing and commitment play a big part. If a would-be mentor doesn't have time for you, then smile graciously and move on. This is one of the downsides of a scenario in which you're formally assigned a mentor: the connection can be kismet, but it isn't always. If it's not, take ownership of that and seek out a better fit.

Rachael

I often describe my first year in principalship as the worst year of my life. As harsh as that may seem, I am just being real, folks. I was twenty-nine and a brand new principal without any additional support in the office. I had relocated to a new part of the state with a student demographic that was unfamiliar, and on top of that, I was going through a divorce. Can you say "fun time"? Not even close! While I do say that it was the worst year of my life, I should also note that it was one of the most rewarding and perhaps the most growth-filled for me, as well. I found ways to overcome the challenges I encountered, and we triumphed as a building. Student growth rates reached an all-time high, and a school once "satisfactory" rated moved up to "outstanding," the highest level designated by the state.

So, how did it all happen? I started by finding a few colleagues whom I could trust, and who had skillfully achieved success in their buildings. These first advisors ended up being the two other middle school principals in my district. Multiple times a week, I would be in a meeting where I didn't know what to do. I would excuse myself to "use the restroom" or "check on something," but in reality, I would be making a phone call in the neighboring conference room or on my cell in the bathroom. I remember calling both of these principals, telling them the situation in a hushed tone and frantically asking for their advice.

Looking back, I am so lucky that both of these educators would answer the phone, give me sentence frames or starters for what to say, and then share a few supportive and encouraging words to boost my confidence. Those first years are hard (okay, let's be honest—every year is hard). We often wonder if we are doing the right thing or are in the right position, so this kind of feedback and positive support can go a long way in encouraging us to keep persevering.

During this first year, our local leaders set up a formal mentoring system with the various directors at the central office and the local education service district. While this program was well intentioned, it presented challenges for me as the year progressed. By the end of the year, the "official" mentoring felt overwhelming and ineffective, and I was looking forward to its end. On the other hand, the unofficial mentors helped me navigate challenges and celebrate successes, which led to my growth as a principal. In the end, this experience made me realize that mentorship is critically important to growth, but "one mentor does not fit all," and too many mentors can be just as tough as having no mentors at all.

Over the years, our mentors have changed as we have grown as administrators and as we've moved building levels and/or districts. Regardless, we have a solid group of folks that we trust and keep close. These people come from our own school districts, professional organizations, and social media. They are both within the education industry and outside of our profession. They are people we can bounce ideas off of, collaborate with, or ask for advice and feedback. Having good mentors has been a game-changer for us professionally, and we're confident it can be for you, too.

INVITATION TO IMPLEMENT

- Narrow down your list of nine to your top three mentor candidates. Remember, you may have to go through several people to find "your people."
  - Colleague-mentor:
  - Professional network mentor:
  - Ugly cry mentor:
- Reach out! See if you can get together for coffee or, if you're in different locations, find a time for a video chat.
- Establish a standing monthly date with at least one of your mentors. We all get so busy that having a standing date on the calendar helps with making mentor time a priority.

CHAPTER THREE

RECEIVE FEEDBACK WITH STYLE

"You can't achieve excellence in life if you fear opinion."

—Janna Cachola

*H*ave you ever walked down the hallway at your school, and when someone asks, "How are you doing?" You flash a wide, toothy grin and say, "Fine!" even when what you really want to say is "Well, actually, my day has been really horrible and I'm considering going into real estate. Two substitute positions weren't filled, and I have to find coverage. A parent who was upset called expressing her displeasure that she couldn't send her child back because she didn't have a doctor's note for that nasty rash, and she's calling the superintendent to complain. I've just reassured a class that it is safe to go back after a room clear due to a student throwing a chair, and the teacher, who happens to be the building union rep, has informed me that she is filing a grievance. On top of all that, I was supposed to get three observations accomplished this morning and . . ."

Yeah, you are not fine. You're overwhelmed, fanatically frazzled, and, quite frankly, feeling completely incompetent. Why didn't the professors in your administration program teach you how to deal with the enormity of all *this*? And why did no one ever tell you you'd have to deal with all of this *this-ness* in the same morning? So, what do you do? You've signed the principal contract, so you're definitely committed. Let's turn that commitment to positive action!

Why is it that some leaders make it look so easy, and some of us can barely get through cafeteria duty without eating a pound of chocolate? We'll tell you right now, friends: No matter how many years you have done this job, it is never easy. However, what distinguishes the successful leaders from those of us who are flailing and flustered is that they're able to recognize—and incorporate—feedback.

Feedback. What a scary word, regardless of whether you are a principal, building leader, district office boss—or just human! We all knew it would be hard and that there would be a huge learning curve, but none of us really knew how big that curve would be until we were in the middle of it, barely hanging on. After all, when you already feel like you are sinking, why on earth would you ask anyone to confirm your worst fears that you're a huge failure and a fraud? That doesn't sound like fun. However, if you can get over this fear and conquer the insecure voice in your head that launches you into a self-loathing dither, you will be able to recognize that feedback can provide you with an incredible opportunity for growth.

> We all knew it would be hard and that there would be a huge learning curve, but none of us really knew how big that curve would be until we were in the middle of it, barely hanging on.

Rachael

One year, the administrators in the district I was working in were directed to give an anonymous survey about their performance and leadership, at each of their buildings, multiple times throughout the year. While the idea of the anonymous survey was good, in practice it yielded some confusion on my end. By nature, I am a fixer, and I often need clarification to make sure I am understanding things correctly. That's hard to do when you don't know whom to ask.

Over the years, I have tried my hand at surveys with names attached, anonymous surveys, open discussions as an entire staff, and open door policies. While each of these formats gave me useful feedback, I still felt like I was missing something. Recently, while keeping up with these various feedback tools, I added one-on-one meetings with each staff member, which occur throughout the year. This tweak has yielded a wealth of useful information and feedback. I work to keep the conversation positive by asking about things my staff members are proud of, plans they're making for the coming months, and how I can help them with their projects. I wrap up the conversation by asking how I could improve. I share with them my desire to always be growing as a leader and the fact that feedback is an important part of this process. I often explain to the new folks who haven't done one of these meetings with me before how face-to-face feedback really helps me understand the nature of a situation and lets me seek clarification when it's needed. The response from staff has been incredible, and I've found that I've been able to identify and then work through trends in the feedback.

Although it's sometimes difficult to navigate, deep down we all know feedback is crucial in our daily lives. As we mentioned previously, education researcher John Hattie has done meta-analysis studies on factors influencing student achievement and growth rates. The impact of feedback is arguably the most critical and powerful aspect of teaching and learning. Therefore, it is not surprising that successful principals become masterful at both giving and receiving feedback in a variety of ways.

Feedback comes to us at various times and in the most peculiar ways, but sometimes you'll need to go looking for it. Why wait until you get your state assessment scores back or your end-of-year evaluation from your boss? Although these two sources do provide significant information, these forms of feedback are more like an autopsy, with little opportunity to change immediate outcomes. What you need, especially when starting out, is a tool that helps keep your community alive and thriving. In fact, if you are solely relying on these two pieces of information as feedback and using that to drive your change, you won't be able to optimize your growth. To gain immediate and timely results, you need feedback early and often so you can respond to the overall needs of your students, staff, and community.

So, how can you get this feedback? Some of the most impactful feedback comes to us by simply listening and watching. The number of greetings being said up and down the hallway can tell us about school culture. Climbing to the top of the jungle gym and watching how students interact (or don't interact) with each other can give us a glimpse into how our community embraces inclusion. Riding the bus home with our students and seeing their neighborhoods can provide endless insights into how to support their needs in ways that go far beyond academics.

Beyond your students, you have the golden opportunity to capitalize on an amazing resource for feedback: your staff! Give them the opportunity and vehicle to provide feedback proactively. While the norm at our schools is to praise publicly and constructively criticize privately, there is always the potential to get "zinged" publicly. One way to increase positive relationships and buy-in while decreasing negativity and disengagement is to make sure you have staff members who may be disgruntled or disenfranchised in your regular feedback loop. (And yes, you can trust that whatever's not given a chance to be shared with you directly is being shared behind your back.)

We all know those scowling people with their arms crossed at the back of the room as you share your latest and greatest idea. At any given moment, they may choose to be on your team or not. Though it's tempting in these settings to gravitate toward your positive supporters and ignore the pulsing negativity from the back, consider going toward the dark side to find enlightenment. Instead of glossing over or avoiding the opinions of people who you may find contrary, unpleasant, or negative, dip in and learn the "why" behind their actions. Some of your greatest growth just might come from the people at the back table.

> Instead of glossing over or avoiding the opinions of people who you may find contrary, unpleasant, or negative, dip in and learn the "why" behind their actions.

Homing in on the feedback process through calculated conversations can elicit a whole new pathway to constructive criticism. Those we might have brushed off as being irrational, always upset, or lacking credibility suddenly have merit. Not that their feedback didn't have value before; it's that the clarifying questions, used to determine the "how" and "why," bring deeper understanding. Making time for these difficult conversations will help us understand various perspectives, what impacts these viewpoints, and how this relates to our school community.

One exercise that can be helpful is to make a feedback web. In the center of the web, put your name. Start by drawing lines out from your name, and in a bubble at the end of each line, write a topic that is important for you to receive feedback on. For example, at the end points, you could have school culture, staff-meeting effectiveness, equity of handling student management, feedback given on observations, differentiated practices, etc. Under each of the topics, write the names of people who could give you valuable feedback. Remember, varying your stakeholders will increase the likelihood you'll obtain a full picture. Go beyond the logical choices. In addition to asking your staff, branch out and ask students, parents, neighbors, community partners, district office visitors, and even the mail carrier.

Feedback Web

Sean: Parent that comes to school often

Amy: Itinerant staff that works in multiple buildings

Julis: Parent that doesn't come to school often

Ofilia: New student

John: District information/ data person

Clarise: Parent of color

Raysean: Student of color

Positive Culture

Equity of Student Management

Molly

Observation Feedback

Professional Learning

Jason: Classroom teacher

Leah: Instructional assistant

Eric: Music teacher

Jan: Fifth-grade teacher

Staci: Kindergarten teacher

Amy: Special education teacher

Eva: Instructional assistant

An Opportunity for You

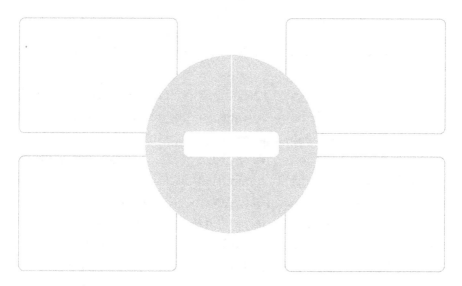

A few years back, Rachael was introduced to the book *Thanks for the Feedback: The Science and Art of Receiving Feedback Well*. It wasn't something that she found perusing Amazon's best-seller list; rather, one of her supervisors suggested her team read it. At the time, she was not sure how to take this suggestion, but she's a sucker for books, so they read up. (Who knows, perhaps the book suggestion was the supervisor's way of providing feedback.) It had a profound impact on her team's practice. The ways in which they responded to feedback, how they received it with their body language, how they processed it, and how they went about soliciting more of it were changed forever. Who knew that feedback could be so complex and impact our work so significantly?!

Seeking out feedback is just the first step in growth, so get ready to put your big-leader boots on! Once you do seek it out, you have to be ready to receive it and to be able to humbly listen to it. We have found that while feedback has the potential to guide us to growth, it also can be hard to hear. One of the most damaging things you can do is to ask someone for their input and then either ignore it or refute it. So, if you are asking for feedback, be ready to listen and take action. Have some clarifying questions ready so you fully understand perspectives that may differ than your own. Proactively formulating questions helps us to avoid jumping to conclusions and becoming defensive. Below are some of our favorite questions that help us accept feedback with grace.

> **Can you tell me more?**
> **Talk to me about _____.**
> **What might that ideally look like?**
> **What do you mean by _____?**
> **How might you approach _____ if you were in a similar situation?**
> **Can you give me an example of _____?**

Keep in mind that you don't have to "win," nor do you have to be "defeated." Just listen, seek clarification, and learn. Understanding this concept makes all the difference, and can lighten the load in an otherwise fraught situation.

Feedback is about learning, so be curious about it. Don't avoid it or pretend it doesn't exist. Once you come to terms with this notion, the meetings with the parent who is steaming with anger or with the teacher that likes to complain will become less stressful, and not so personal. Instead of sitting across the table and feeling attacked, sit side by side and ask responsive questions. No longer scared of what others might say, you will find yourself in a place of growth that will have a positive impact on your practice as a professional. You won't avoid uncomfortable conversations, but instead seek them out on a regular basis. In fact, you just might find the courage to schedule them regularly with some of your harshest critics.

Kate

Relationships with unions and administrators can traditionally be perceived as contentious. In fact, some administrators may even be told when hired that they have gone over to the "dark side," implying that becoming an administrator is something sinister and unsavory. I remember wondering when I first became a principal why there was hostility when we were all in the business of educating and supporting students. I had certainly never had these feelings for my past administrators and was shocked that someone might feel that way about me. I'd like to think that I am my staff's greatest advocate, and that we are not on opposing sides.

In my first few years as a principal, I just assumed that if one of my staff members had a problem with me, or the union was upset with a decision I had made, they would waltz right down to my office and give me feedback. Then, I would empathetically embrace their feedback, and they would waltz back out of my office. After all, I perceived myself as approachable and not intimidating, so why wouldn't others feel the same way? And while I had a few staff members that did give me feedback, I didn't hear much from my union representatives, so I thought everything was going stupendously well. (Have I mentioned that I am a bit of a Pollyanna who tries to see the best in every situation?)

Well, you guessed it: one spring early in my principal career, this Pollyanna's world came crashing down when I learned that a couple of my staff members had gone to human resources to complain about my leadership. To say that I was crushed was an understatement. I remember crumbling in a puddle of tears, not because of the feedback that I was receiving, but because I truly didn't understand why they didn't feel comfortable coming to me personally instead of going to human resources.

Although I was smarting from this dose of reality, I knew I needed to do something different so that my union leadership had a systematic way to give me feedback, rather than feeling their only choice was to go to human resources. This was when I first started monthly feedback sessions with my school union reps. Once a month, I now faithfully meet with the two building reps. We have a consistent meeting protocol that we follow each time we meet. We start every meeting by discussing what is going well within our community, and then we move into concerns and growth opportunities. We also talk about how we can proactively solve problems and continually create a more supportive, productive, and harmonious culture together. We discuss how to communicate with stakeholders and give feedback on how to support one another. I genuinely look forward to these meetings and feel sincere collegiality and trust between us. And while I realistically know that I don't hear all the talk swirling around the halls, I do feel that by implementing systems for feedback, there is more direct transparency and proactive conversation around how we can work together to create a healthy community.

Think for a moment about how you are going to intentionally seek out feedback on a consistent basis. Who are you going to connect with and how? Are you going to meet face-to-face with people, or are you going to create a leadership team? How will you elicit feedback? Will you ask your community to take a survey? How will you analyze and apply the results? We also encourage you to think about how often you will seek out feedback from others. Everything's better with a plan, so let's make one together. Fill out the graphic organizer below to support reflection on feedback.

Sample Feedback Plan

Who will you connect with?	How will you elicit feedback?	What's your timeline?	How will you analyze and apply the results?
Mentor	Send plan for staff meeting (slides, handouts, etc.)	Before our weekly meeting	Implement changes she suggests
Teaching staff	Ask questions about staff morale and workload expectations	Intentional conversations during professional learning teams	Notice trends and brainstorm solutions with leadership team
Union representative	Ask questions about the implementation of new behavior protocols	Standing meeting once a month	Take notes to climate/behavior committee

An Opportunity for You

Who will you connect with?	How will you elicit feedback?	What's your timeline?	How will you analyze and apply the results?

Let's be honest, on any given day, we take in and digest an enormous amount of feedback. It can be difficult to hear, let alone to sift through and compartmentalize in order to make way for positive change. Like anything, making the most of this information takes practice. The more you practice something effectively (notice I did not say "*just* practice"), the more skillful you'll become at it.

Kourtney

As we think about the art of receiving feedback and the ways we can lean into hearing hard messages with open hearts, we need to create the same conditions for our staff when we are giving feedback. It is cringy for me to think back to when I was new in my role of observing teachers as an instructional coach, and how my post-observation conferences were filled with my voice rather than the teacher's. As administrators, we give feedback, both formal and informal, incessantly, but the key lies in giving it in such a way that it will be heard and spark a change. I once came across a brilliant quote about feedback from education researcher Doug Reeves that has stuck with me: "It's not about the feedback given, it's about the feedback received." Mic drop.

When I was first starting out, my method for giving feedback wasn't very effective. The reason was simple: I was doing my thinking in isolation. Polly Patrick, another one of my favorite education gurus, often says, "Whoever is doing the thinking is doing the learning." If I wanted to inspire insight, my teachers and I would have to do the thinking together. I stopped staying up late at night writing beautiful paragraphs of feedback on evaluations and reimagined my approach. Granted, you can't throw all the paperwork out the window, but paperwork isn't going to move the ship. The conversations will.

I would begin each post-observation meeting with questions: What went well? How did you know your students were learning? Can you tell me more about this part? After I was able to get a sense of the teacher's perspective, I could then align my observations to their insights and ask questions to move their thinking: "Hey, we've been talking a lot about student engagement, and I noticed that the group you were working with was really on it. How do we get that same level of engagement at the independent station?" Whether it is losing weight or improving instruction, people change through enhancing their strengths and building on their successes, far more than by identifying and focusing on their weaknesses. With this kind of a model, the post-observations became centered around collaboration, problem-solving, and solution-seeking. My best advice: Be the lead asker, not the expert.

INVITATION TO IMPLEMENT

Think of three people you can trust to give you honest feedback. Consider questions that will get to the core of the information you are seeking.

- How are you going to seek input?
    - Who are you going to connect with and how?
    - Are you going to meet face-to-face, or will you create a leadership team?
    - Will you ask your community to take a survey?

- What's the frequency with which you are going to gather insights?
- What is the intention of seeking feedback?
- Craft a conversation and practice with a mentor using the below prompts:
    - Can you tell me more?
    - Talk to me about _____.
    - What might that ideally look like?
    - What do you mean by _____?
    - How might you approach _____ if you were in a similar situation?
    - Can you give me an example of _____?

— PART TWO —

FOCUS

CHAPTER FOUR

CLARIFY YOUR PURPOSE

"Yes, in all my research, the greatest leaders looked inward and were able to tell a good story with authenticity and passion."

—Deepak Chopra

*Y*ou have only been on the job for one month, and already you have a list a mile long with all the things that need to be changed, updated, fixed, or addressed throughout the building. The student study team hasn't been following the right process to refer students to special education—that needs to be fixed before a lawsuit creeps across your desk. The novice teacher who needs support looking at data, and instead thinks vocabulary should be mastered by copying words and definitions from a dictionary. Where is my Tylenol? The office staff is still operating with paper schedules, paper attendance, paper sign-in sheets, and paper timecards—and they still use a typewriter. Yep, we have some technology updates to implement in the future. It might feel that every time you turn around, you find yourself venturing deeper into a cave of archaic systems, structures, practices, and traditions. Soon, you are comparing yourself to an archeologist: occasionally uncovering treasures, but having to sift through a lot of dirt to obtain them. Phew! There is a lot of work to do, and where do you start?

Ask anyone who has worked for an ineffective principal, and you will start to notice themes of inconsistency, distrust, favoritism, lack of follow through, low visibility, and game playing. Frankly, nothing tanks morale faster. On the other hand, a leader who understands their purpose with clarity and vision, who has the ability to lead with authenticity, is like a breath of fresh air. Their "why" is communicated clearly and consistently to staff, parents, students, and the community. When decisions come down that may be unpopular, they are also grounded in this authenticity and clarity so that others can understand their reasoning.

One of the things that connected the three of us as friends and colleagues so quickly was that our "whys" were so aligned. We felt drawn to be allies for students and families that are experiencing poverty, oppressed by systemic racism, and affected by the opportunity gap. We believe deeply in the potential for each child to grow and achieve. We are relentless in the pursuit of student success. We also understand and accept that our staff has the ability to leverage the things we as adults control in order to maximize outcomes for students.

Achieving authentic leadership requires some deep soul-searching, and clarity of purpose makes all the difference between mediocre leaders and exceptional ones. When leaders are grounded in their purpose, they view everything that comes their way through the lens of their educational beliefs and vision. This guides their decisions big and small, and also helps them inspire others and create a collective community that is moving in the same direction for all kids.

Why did you choose this job? What made you want to do this work? If your first answer

> When leaders are grounded in their purpose, they view everything that comes their way through the lens of their educational beliefs and vision.

is money, believe us there are easier ways to make it. You chose this incredibly challenging path for a reason.

You will know that you have landed on your purpose when you can not only articulate it, but you feel it in your bones. This grounding is important. Your "why" is a combination of your passion, your philosophy, your beliefs, your motivation, and the legacy you want to leave behind.

Don't underestimate the power of the elevator speech. In your role, you will constantly be engaging in brief conversations with others, from staff to students, parents to community members, where this sound bite will be essential. At the end of the day, you may not remember the interaction, but chances are, *they* will, and you want them to remember what you stand for. You want to be able to clearly and concisely articulate your passion and purpose for the work you do in your school. The better you are able to do this, the stronger your impact will be.

As you unwrap your purpose, consider asking yourself the following guiding questions and journaling your responses.

- Why did I go into education?
- What parts of that initial motivation have stayed with me?
- When do I feel most aligned with my core beliefs?
- What makes my work meaningful?
- How could I use this motivation to amplify the impact on students?

Once you have recorded your initial thoughts, a great exercise is to distill your words down to a short sentence or an elevator speech of about five to six sentences that articulates your "why." This becomes the launching point for communicating your purpose to others.

It is critically important to also create a shared vision with your teachers and staff members. As you are working to strengthen the culture of your building, it would be smart to take them through a similar exercise to identify their purpose and motivation for the work they do. The first step is to set aside a time or times where you can move together through progressive questions, reflection, and safe sharing.

Listen carefully as they share from the heart. Through dialogue and conversation, your team has the opportunity to identify its collective vision, and out of this work, taglines or mottos may emerge. For example, three that we us use at our schools are: "Growing All Kids," "Rigor and Joy," and "Everyone Growing." These tag lines become the touchstones for the work you will do as a group. The focus from individual egos to the powerful "we" shifts as the group does something bigger than themselves. The words that become your touchstone illustrate the impact this group of educators will have as they align their individual purposes to their intentions for the students they serve. And, as a school leader, this work begins with you. You activate a powerhouse of collective efficacy by honestly sharing your "why" for the work. This requires vulnerability, authenticity, passion, and clarity that might make your voice quiver a little as you speak. If it does, go with it. It means you are on the right path.

————————————— *Kourtney* —————————————

I chose to be a principal because principals have the opportunity to change the trajectory of kids' lives. My "why" for this work is deeply grounded in social justice and a relentless belief that all kids can grow. I didn't come into education directly; my love for this work started at San Quentin State Prison in the late nineties, when I was attending college at University of San Francisco. I was volunteering in the Catholic chapel at the prison with a priest from my college, who was offering a course and happened to need a teaching assistant. We had a full class of mostly lifers who had done horrendous crimes. I expected our students to be a scary bunch of hardened criminals. What I found instead was a group of bright men, almost entirely people of color who came from poverty, many of whom were immigrants from war-torn countries. They had frequently had disruptions in their education, and had found community and power through gangs, violence, and drugs. In hearing their stories, I felt in my bones that had their educational experiences been different, they might have had some agency and empowerment to go a different way.

A principal changed the trajectory for my own family. In 1960, my mom found herself pregnant while she was in high school. In those days, it was expected that she drop out of school. She wasn't allowed to attend during the day, as she would be a bad influence on the other girls. My grandparents forced her to get married and planned for her to stop her education. Her principal changed all that. He contacted my grandparents and told them that she was too talented to stop learning. He wanted to offer something bold: an opportunity for her to return in the evenings after the other students had left, so she could keep up with her classes. Despite the fact that my mom had two babies by the time she was nineteen, she graduated high school with high marks. She went on to be the first in her family to go to college and had an incredible career as a nurse manager. This happened because an educator made a decision to believe in her potential.

School administrators have the power to remove obstacles and barriers in order to promote equity in ways that can shift entire futures, not just for the student at hand, but their children and children's children. So much of the work is laborious, sure, but man, not many other professions can say the same. It gets me out of bed every day, it heightens my expectations, and it grounds me in my resolve to continue that relentless pursuit in the belief that every child has an unlimited capacity to learn.

If you and your staff are on a climb to excellence, it's up to you as a leader to hike to the top of the next hill so you can see the big picture and point the way ahead. There are times in the midst of the work when you might stumble, or—let's be honest—be pushed down the hill into the weeds, but your job is to climb back up to the top of the hill as quickly as possible to make sure you're moving in the right direction. A leader who lives in the weeds ignores the most important part of the work: maintaining focus and progressing toward the goal.

Make sure that your purpose is both lofty and worthy. Higher test scores are not inspirational, and yet we know that children and adolescents need academic success to open the doors of opportunity.

Providing students with a strong foundation so they can have a better life is inspirational. Consider the hope and promise for the future of your students, and consider disrupting systems that haven't worked for all students. As a strong instructional leader, your clarity of purpose becomes the thread that weaves through everything you touch, from instructional programming, to master scheduling, to the importance you give to the mundane managerial tasks that are also requirements of the job.

Rachael

"We knew it was bad, but not this bad!" That was how my first day as an elementary principal started, as the recent state report card data came flying across the table at me. Apparently, for a variety of reasons, the year before I arrived had been really hard, and state assessment scores and growth rates for all students dropped to an all-time low. In fact, it landed our building in the lowest 10 percent of Oregon elementary schools when you factored in our achievement levels, overall growth rates in reading and math, and growth rates of our special populations. When I tried to learn from the staff what had happened, I got a lot of shrugs and comments about how it was just bad, like, really bad. We started trying to find our way forward when we didn't really even know how we got lost. It was challenging, to say the least.

For the first few months, I did a lot of listening. I met with my entire staff, either in small groups or one-on-one. I was in classrooms every day. Near the end of the second month, we started to have meetings about our "why" and the purpose of the work we were doing for kids. The staff members each shared their purpose to each other, to grade levels, and to the entire staff. Commonalities started to arise, where folks were talking about supporting kids, growing them, and helping them reach unknown heights. We agreed that the students' time at school was something we could shape, no matter what.

Once we knew our "why," we had to figure out how we were going to move the needle when it came to growth. Three themes emerged: academics, attitude, and attendance. These were the three things the staff always talked about in the hallways, classrooms, lunch room, and office. When I shared these observations, they all started nodding in agreement. This was it. This was how we were going to grow kids. If kids were here at school, they could learn. If we could get behavior under control and consistent management practices in place, teachers could teach. And if teachers could teach, we knew without a doubt that kids would learn. We just knew it!

Now that we had our focus aligned to growing all students through academics, attitude, and attendance, we had to figure out what we needed to take off our plate and what needed to stay. We took time to see how each task, event, system, and structure was aligned to our shared mission of growing kids. By the time winter break rolled around, we had reduced our focus to only those things we believed truly added to our goal of enriching all students.

This exercise is something we come back to each year, to specifically align our actions and professional development to the work we are doing for kids. By explicitly talking about growing all kids and our "three As," and by reexamining our focus consistently as a team, it helps keep our vision and focus sharp and accurate, year after year. After all, our building didn't want to be a jack-of-all-trades and a master of none.

Years later, we are still focusing on accelerating student growth through academics, attitude, and attendance. Our growth rates are now some of the highest in the state, and our special populations are rocking it. We moved from being one of the lowest performing elementary schools in Oregon to now outperforming 80 percent of them. That's the power of purpose.

COMMUNICATING YOUR PURPOSE

As a leader, you are the chief storyteller of your school; communicating the journey to your community. It is important to keep your clarity of purpose front and center in your newsletters, emails, and social media. So many principals miss this chance by delegating community communication to support staff. The newsletters and messages sent home tend to become focused simply on the nuts and bolts of the school. Don't let that happen. Think about the impact you might have if you send out the conference schedule with a few lines about why conferences connect to your vision for student success. Instead of only posting reminders about events on Facebook, consider snapping a picture of teachers collaborating and describe their passion for student success. Every communication is an opportunity to paint a clearer picture of your school's vision and keep student success at the forefront. When you are intentional about communicating the purpose of your leadership with every interaction, it becomes the anchor that holds you steady.

Consider this: companies brand and rebrand themselves all the time. Why should it be any different with our schools? To help build energy around your school's purpose, create a new school logo, get swag with your school motto emblazoned on it, highlight your purpose on your reader board, and add your mantra under your signature in emails. Perhaps have a poster-making contest that invites students to illuminate your shared vision, or create a song that incorporates your values for your spirit assemblies. There are dozens of creative ways to get your positive message out there.

You might begin this work by reflecting on the reputation of your school and community. All of us have reputations. Some of these reputations are grounded in facts, while others are developed through gossip and assumptions. One thing is for certain: our school, district, or own personal story will undoubtedly be told. Ultimately, you have the power to influence that story. Instead of having someone else fill in the gaps, take charge and spend time broadcasting your purpose and all the amazing things that your school is achieving. Plaster your newsletters and website, Facebook, or Twitter account with positive words and pictures. While you have a captive audience at one of your music or sporting events, take the opportunity to share something positive happening in your school.

ALIGNING PURPOSE WITH ACTION

A strong clarity of purpose helps you make decisions. In the last chapter, we discussed the ways that feedback can be cultivated and curated to strengthen your impact. Clarity of purpose, then, helps you know how to prioritize, align, and move forward. Are you overwhelmed thinking about everything on your plate? Not to worry. Below, we've included a tool to help you assess what things are more and less aligned with your school vision.

As you consider the tasks and demands in your average day, filter them in order to prioritize. Identify what has to get done each day (essential), what's nice to get each day (optional), and how connected each of these activities is to your long-term purpose. Do you remember how your inbox suddenly filled up when you became principal? How you were inundated by opportunities for professional development, guest speakers, field trips, furniture, online curricula—you name it? Whatever it is, you've gotten at least 4,789 emails about it. Hidden among the junk might be a gem, but do you read every single email to find it? No way. That same skill we have learned through dealing with too much email can be used for prioritizing initiatives and systems in our work. It is not uncommon for a busy administrator to have a daunting to-do list with fifty competing priorities. The tool below can help to prioritize these items by identifying how they align with your vision and whether or not they are essential to get done.

Example: Analyzing and Your To-Do List

Aligned to Our Vision		
	Weakly Aligned	**Strongly Aligned**
Essential	• Processing behavior referrals • Completing a state report • Returning phone call from community member • Sifting through inbox (SCHEDULE a time to do these.)	• Giving feedback to data teams • Creating professional development • Recognizing staff • Scheduling post observation conferences • Creating schedule that maximizes instruction (PRIORITIZE these first.)
Optional	Scheduling an assembly Organizing and color coding files (DELEGATE these tasks.)	• Reviewing curriculum for next year • Researching master schedule alternatives • Updating the parent website (PLAN to do these at a less urgent time.)

An Opportunity for You

Aligned to Our Vision		
	Weakly Aligned	**Strongly Aligned**
Essential		
Optional		

Authenticity in leadership means knowing at your core what you believe and what you stand for. By creating a culture where cultivating clarity of purpose becomes how you do business, you will gain ground quicker and more efficiently. Choosing to do this work means choosing to invest in being proactive rather than reactive.

Kate

When I first started out, I was "that principal"; the one who wanted to try everything all at once. I'd hear an idea at a conference and want to implement it the next day. Data at another building was skyrocketing, so I grabbed onto their vision and hurled it to our staff. An article would detail the latest trend, and I would make copies and put it in the teachers' boxes, eager to see the concepts miraculously transferred into their classrooms the next week. My good intentions led to a totally overwhelmed staff that didn't know which way to go. Why? Their leader didn't think about how all these ideas fit in our existing system or contributed to our goals. Think about how a puppy would lead school improvement, and that was basically me.

I'll never forget the first year I led the staff in writing our school improvement plan. I set up rotating stations for staff members to brainstorm ideas. At the end of the staff input time, we had dozens and dozens of ideas of how we could improve our school outcomes. Some ideas were lofty, and some were one-and-done activities. They all seemed pretty good to me, so we wrote *all of them* into our plan. (I can feel you shaking your head as you read this.) I proudly presented our thirty-eight-page school improvement plan to the district office, foolishly thinking that more equaled better. Oh, Kate . . .

Not surprisingly, our plan led to confusion, frustration, and apathy, because we had no clarity of purpose. I was not grounded in my "why," and I certainly could not strategically link our activities to a common vision.

As my years as a principal have progressed, I have gravitated toward the "go deep" concept for school improvement and have left the shallowness of that thirty-eight-page plan behind. Focusing on no more than three or four school-wide goals has allowed our staff to implement with purpose, fidelity, and laser focus. It has made a significant difference in not only student achievement, but also staff morale.

I do still fight the urge to bring back the latest and greatest ideas from conferences and to arbitrarily try new things with my staff and students without linking them to our common goals. However, I am mindful that this is a weak spot for me, and I have surrounded myself with people who remind me of the "why" behind our vision. Even after almost two decades of being a principal, this old dog is still learning new tricks.

INVITATION TO IMPLEMENT

- What do you stand for? Identify the "why" and purpose for both you and your building.
    - What are your nonnegotiables?
    - What are your mission and vision?
    - What are your beliefs about learners?
    - What is your overall school goal?
    - What is the data telling you?
    - What originally drew you to this work?
- Communicate it! Make a plan for how you are going to communicate and brand your school's purpose to all stakeholders.

CHAPTER FIVE

DECIDE TO GO DEEP

"People think focus means saying yes to the thing you've got to focus on. But that's not what it means at all. It means saying no to the hundred other good ideas that there are. You have to pick carefully."

–Steve Jobs

*I*t is the end of September, and your assessment teams have been diligently assessing your students to gather information so you can make informed decisions. You marvel at their heroic patience in listening to the same passage read over and over again, out in a stuffy hallway. You and your leadership team have created a rainbow of an assessment wall that shows data for every student, their strengths, and their areas of focus. There is so much information to digest on those tiny assessment cards, and it is hard to figure out where to start. Each chart, graph, and progress-monitoring notebook is pulsating with areas of triumph to be celebrated and areas of need that require growing. The data is beckoning you to react, and you know how much differentiation needs to happen with your students, staff, and families. The desire to do it all, right now, pulls you in different directions. A wave of indecision knocks you flat, and you don't know how to move forward. Do you start with your core systems or intervention block? Should you bring in a presenter, or should you do a book study with the staff to learn engagement strategies? Do you focus on attendance or behavior or phonics? Ugh . . . there just seem to be too many decisions. How do you know where to start?

With your purpose now firmly in place, it's time to take action. Does that idea terrify you? Energize you? Maybe a bit of both? The good news is that school improvement is not all that complex. As we discussed earlier, it may not be easy, but it's not that complicated if you have consistent systems and structures to support your vision. There are a few critical questions that will help get you started. At any given time, you and your teachers should be able to answer these questions about every student in your care:

- What is the data telling you about your students' learning?
- How is the staff using the standards for instruction?
- What strategies are being used to teach the standards?
- Are your students growing? How do you know?
- How does it feel to be at school?

WHAT IS THE DATA TELLING YOU?

The three of us are all self-proclaimed data nerds. Call us wacky, but nothing beats pouring over the latest progress-monitoring reports to see which students have grown, stagnated, or slipped. It is like each student is a mystery, and each piece of data is a clue to unlocking them. To make well-informed decisions, it is important to look at a variety of assessments. Information from state test scores, building-wide data, classroom-based measures, and individual performance in daily classwork all help with giving a clear picture of each student. However, data doesn't always have to be academic. It is important to know your students' behavioral and attendance data. Both of these sources of information can give you a wealth of knowledge about why they may be succeeding or struggling academically. As you sift through the data, we encourage you to examine it from the following viewpoints: as a building, as a grade level, as a cohort of students, as a classroom, and as an individual student at their level. Dive into the story behind the data to bring enlightenment to the surface.

ARE YOU USING STANDARDS?

Standards are the foundation of teaching. If you are striving for equity among your teachers, they must be teaching from your state and/or district standards. Our students deserve to be taught what is intended to be taught for their subject or grade level. We know that standards are kind of technical, but they are necessary blueprints to ensure equity of outcomes. They should be present at every planning session and infused into every lesson. Your teachers might want to teach their favorite penguin unit they have taught for the past twenty-five years, but unless they can show you that the project relates back to their designated standards, you'll need to put the kibosh on it. We know this sounds harsh, but we never have enough time to teach all that is required, so bring out the tough love and ask the hard questions about how the lessons are connected to the standards. Yes, we think students should have fun at school, and we also believe educators can create engaging and enjoyable lessons grounded in their grade level's standards.

STRATEGIES ARE THE NAME OF THE GAME

Curricula will come and go, but effective strategies are forever! We truly believe selecting the right materials is important and something you should research before purchasing. Although we love a curriculum that has pretty pictures and glossy covers and all the "stuff," look deeper at how publishers infuse the materials with strategies. It is important to note that strategies connect the curriculum to the students, and without them, the curriculum is meaningless.

As you go deep, select two or three strategies that all your staff can learn and use to connect to the curriculum, no matter what content area they are teaching. Even if you are teaching social studies, home economics, math, art, or PE, these are strategies that all staff can use. For example, one of our favorite strategies is "number of opportunities to respond." This is an engagement strategy that gets great results. Engagement equals doing! We want our students to interact with the curriculum, not just "sit and get" the material from the instructor. Ask yourself: How many students are engaged when a teacher calls on one student? Yes, you got it: ONE! Therefore, have your teachers learn how to incorporate "doing" with as many students as possible and into as many of their lessons as possible. The number of opportunities to respond strategy could come in the form of choral responses, turn and talk, structured partnerships, total-body responses or physical responses like thumbs up, writing on a small whiteboard and holding up the answer, cooperative learning, or group work with assigned roles.

Whichever strategy you choose, always be mindful that as leaders we must teach, model, reinforce, repeat. We encourage you to first explicitly teach the strategy to your staff. Take the time to differentiate with your staff who may have the strategy mastered or those that might need some additional support. Undoubtedly, you already have awesome staff members who are incorporating the selected strategy into their lessons, so ask them if they would be willing to co-present or host their peers in their classroom so others can see it in action. Most of life's lessons are caught and not taught, so model your chosen strategy in your own staff meetings. You might also look for ways to keep the strategy alive by mentioning it in your weekly announcements. Or, as you are completing your walkthroughs, jot down which teachers are incorporating the strategy and write a quick note commending them on the implementation. This is the perfect opportunity to drop some anchors of appreciation (see p. 179 for more on this), so make sure you are specific and that your note includes details about how their actions are tied to the vision, mission, or "why" of your building. There are dozens of powerful active participation and engagement strategies out there, so pick a few and infuse with purpose them into your school community.

IS EVERYONE GROWING?

Kate's motto at her school is "Everyone Growing." This means the students, the staff, *and* the principal. We all know that the people in our care come to us with various strengths and areas for growth. Our goal is to ensure that everyone is progressing, regardless if they are a student above or below grade level, or a teacher in their first or thirtieth year. As leaders, you must ask yourself this question: Is everyone growing?

> As leaders, you must ask yourself this question: Is everyone growing?

The only way you can answer this is by looking at various disaggregated data points and noticing trends with individual students, staff, and subgroups. Student examples may include gender, race, language, or poverty level. Staff examples may include grade levels, department, or varied teaching experience. We encourage you to track growth data based on the person who is teaching the group, the curriculum that is being used, the time of day, and the number of instructional minutes. Ask yourself why this particular student or staff group is growing exponentially, while another student or staff group is not? When you are examining your growth rates, remember this quote from Dr. Paul Batalden: "Every system is perfectly designed to get the results it gets."

Growth trends can provide the information leaders need to impact decision-making. When students *are* growing, find out what's working and replicate throughout your system. If students are not growing, also find out why, and shift your practices to support their learning. Look at the data and think about why a particular teacher consistently has stellar results. On the flip side, perhaps your instructor is faltering and needs coaching on effective strategies. Maybe instruction is being cut short seven minutes each day because they are coming in late from lunch. Perhaps a group of students is receiving instruction in a loud hallway with lots of distractions. Make this deep dive into the "why" and make changes immediately. It is imperative that we ensure high-quality support and instruction and provide additional instruction to our students who have historically been impacted by the opportunity gap. They don't have time to wait until the state assessment results come in or report cards are sent home to receive optimal instruction. If a change is needed, find a way to do it today. Unpack the reasons and replicate or shift your practice to help your students and staff achieve optimal outcomes.

HOW DOES IT FEEL AT SCHOOL?

We can have the best systems and structures for analyzing data, implementing learning standards, and delivering research-based strategies with the greatest curriculum, but if our kids and staff do not like being at our schools, then we will never make optimal progress. As humans, we need to feel connected, supported, and have a sense of purpose, and it is critical that we also have systems to generate happiness. We have committees that focus on data, curriculum development, and specific interventions. Why not have a Culture Committee that's sole purpose is generating deeper connections and happiness within your building? Gather your stakeholders, including your students, and have a regular monthly meeting. Make the decision to go deep on creating a positive culture where the students and staff can't wait to show up, and we bet your other school improvement efforts will skyrocket, as well.

> As humans, we need to feel connected, supported, and have a sense of purpose, and it is critical that we also have systems to generate happiness.

Rachael

Each year we start off the school year with a deep data dive. We used to do this during in-service week, but through trial and error, we found it was too overwhelming as staff prepared to welcome kids back. Now we do our data dive during the first month, either during our early release or staff meeting time. Regardless of when it's held, we make sure to go through the process as a full staff, as we believe everyone in the building impacts student performance, regardless of the role they play in the school. We are all educators.

As a building, we first start at the thirty-thousand-foot level, and we look at the overall health of the school. How are students performing overall? What was the school's overall growth rate and how did each student subgroup perform? From the school level, we dive into the grade level. We look at each grade level's growth as a cohort from the previous year and their historical records from past years. Again, we dive back into subgroup data, as we want to ensure all of our students are learning at high rates and that no opportunity gaps exist. Once we look at the data from a grade-level perspective, we dive even deeper as we look at it on the class and student levels.

When I first started as a principal, I used to do all the data diving for the staff. They literally just sat there and listened to me talk on and on about the data, and then give my conclusions. Sometimes it went on for two hours. Looking back, I feel so bad for those staff members during my early years. Ironically, it wasn't until I received some feedback that my method wasn't effective, collaborative, or empowering that I changed my approach.

I am happy to share that our data dives are now much more engaging and teacher-centered. As principal, I have the data printed and ready to go for them, and that is about the extent of the role I play in setting things up. Now, instead of me talking at them and doing all the thinking, learning, and ownership, I have staff talk as an entire building or grade level. I provide time for them to dig into the data and then share their findings. The standard guiding questions we use are as simple as:

- What do you see?
- What are some areas of celebration?
- What do you find interesting?
- What "aha" moments might you have?

- What might you ponder as you move forward?
- What support might be needed for students, staff, or others as we move forward?

Over time, I have found that empowering staff to understand and break down the data and process the "why" behind it is so much more meaningful than me doing it all. As you are thinking about what your data might look like, I encourage you to entrust your staff with this process. How can you place them at the center of the conversation?

Our students need us to develop both culture and academic achievement goals, and they can't spend years waiting for you to shore up one at the expense of the other. Strong leaders do both, simultaneously and with intention. We want to care for the social-emotional needs of students and staff as much as we do for their academic learning. A school system is complicated and multifaceted, and though your efforts may feel broad, as you prioritize and work with intention, you'll gain a deeper understanding of how to leverage change. Rather than try to do everything all at once, which will no doubt stretch you and your staff too thin, narrow your focus. As you address both culture and academic achievement, keep the "four C's"— core instruction, collaboration, culture, and communication—at the heart of your implementation.

Core instruction is a clearly articulated system for curriculum, teaching strategies, and the learning environment that ensures equity of experience from one classroom to the next. In any given school, you will find islands of excellence. You know, those teachers who shine no matter what grade, subject, or students they teach. Conversely, you may

> Our students need us to develop both culture and academic achievement goals, and they can't spend years waiting for you to shore up one at the expense of the other.

also have the teacher who always has the lowest performing students, year after year. As leaders, this is heart wrenching because we see the huge disparity. We must acknowledge the inequity and strive to eliminate it by elevating our emergent educators, replicating success, and working to have all our teachers at a performance level where we would fight to have our *own* children, grandchildren, nieces, and nephews in each of their classes. Truly successful schools have created systems of review and refinement that promote equity, and these systems start with core instruction.

Teaching is both an art and a science. Articulating a solid core is about having tight enough expectations and sufficient consistency to ensure all students are learning, while honoring each teacher's style and expertise. Are your instructors teaching to the same standards? Are they using the same materials? Are students learning at the same rate? Are *all* students receiving core grade-level instruction? These are scary questions to ask when core instruction is not in place, because it can be a little like peeling an onion. We encourage you to start with finding the pillars that your team can agree on, like standards, pacing calendars, assessment timelines, and common scoring rubrics. Agreeing on areas of focus to improve outcomes for students will help set the stage for teacher collaboration and student success. As the instructional leader, it is then critically important that you are frequently in the classrooms during core instruction, so you can support your staff and students, while also monitoring the fidelity of implementation.

Culture steeped in support is critical for schools to operate well. This work is deeply personal and can be emotionally taxing, but it's essential. After all, if a school doesn't feel like a safe and welcoming place for adults, there is no way it can feel that way for students. If you have ever worked in a building with a broken culture, you know how awful it can be. The air feels stagnant. You walk down the hallway and see faces void of joy. The staff room is a minefield of negativity and complaints. Staff members feel stifled by the hierarchy. As an administrator, you may not have caused it, but it is your job to help fix it. Culture is not something that can be imposed on a staff, it has to be created alongside them. It starts by engaging in courageous conversations, listening deeply, and noticing the obstacles. Make sure your staff's voices are heard, give them the chance to implement their ideas, and encourage them to be leaders in this collective work. Doing so will help launch the culture into a place of cooperation.

Collaboration is key to school improvement. There's a great scene in the movie *School of Rock* where the kids are all playing instruments out of sync, and the teacher inspires them with the concept of musical fusion and the power of being in sync. The same is true for schools. There are teams that operate like symphonies, and others that might as well be playing air guitar. Creating the conditions for meaningful collaboration can transform student outcomes and enhance the culture of your building. Like any meaningful change, it's best to begin with the end in mind. What do you hope to achieve together? Truly, there is nothing more magical than a group of wickedly smart individuals aligning their practice to better serve kids.

Start by creating a consistent schedule for your teams to collaborate. Think about how you can creatively carve out regular times for them to meet, and put these meetings into your master schedule. Opportunities for collaboration might be found during the following times:

- Early release or late start times
- Common prep times for a grade level
- While having others cover classes to create additional time
- While holding school-wide or grade-level events, such as assemblies, and providing coverage to release teachers to work together
- You may also choose to cancel other meetings to give teachers more time to connect.

Wherever you can find the time, stay faithful to this schedule to show your commitment to collaboration. We all know that if we have a predictable schedule, we are more likely to follow it.

Next, take your teams through a series of questions so they better understand each other. Proactively setting up your teams for success and meeting expectations will save you headaches later. We suggest first bringing all your teams together in one location and having them do some self-reflective writing. Then, have them verbally share with their teammates. Several of our favorite prompts include:

- What do you value when working on a team?
- What is your vision for our team?
- What is something you want people to know about you?
- What items are important to have on our agenda?
- Our team needs support with . . .

Another important step is to establish norms for optimal collaboration. Norms are essentially agreements that keep teams grounded. We suggest teams have five to seven norms that focus on the below:

Time:

- When will we meet?
- Will we set a beginning and ending time?
- Will we start and end on time?

Active Participation:

- How will we encourage listening and discourage interrupting?
- How will we encourage equity of voice?
- How will we stop side conversations?
- What does active participation look and sound like?

Confidentiality:

- Will meetings be open or closed?
- Will what we say in the meeting be held in confidence?
- What can be said after the meeting?

Decision-Making:

- How will we make decisions?
- Will we be an advisory or a decision-making body?
- Will we reach decisions by consensus?

- How will we deal with conflicts?

Expectations:

- What will we expect from members?
- Will there be requirements for participation?

Below are a few examples of norms:

- Everyone has a voice—no interrupting or sidebar conversations.
- An agenda will be communicated twenty-four hours prior to the meeting.
- Roles will be in place before each meeting.
- Our meetings will start and end on time.
- Adequate notice will be given as to when and where the meeting will occur.
- People will stick to the agenda and avoid getting off topic.
- Our meetings will have a purpose with equity of voice.
- Everyone will be present and actively participate.
- Please avoid side conversations.
- Please do not correct papers or do other work during the meetings.
- Everyone will face the speaker.

Communicate thoroughly and strategically. When you've identified your focus areas for school improvement, you'll need to create a plan for communicating them to your team, community, and stakeholders, so that everyone is clear on the priorities. This is when you put on your motivational-speaker hat. As they say, "Go big or go home!" You might consider choosing a quote, mantra, or theme song that energizes staff around your goals. This may be something that makes it crystal clear what you are doing together, why you are doing it, and what you want to achieve as a team. Allow your creativity to shine and infuse your communication with fun and joy.

Every person receives and digests information uniquely, so vary your communication methods. Start out with that motivational speech and then follow up with emails, tweets, notes in mailboxes, and newsletter blurbs. You may even get really creative and create a video to share with your community. Next, spotlight staff and students who are implementing your initiative. For example, you can develop systems for peer observations, create a bulletin board with photos, or write personal cards to share what you've observed, and the next time the superintendent is in the building, take him or her into the classroom and share—in front of the teacher—their amazing efforts. Without a thorough and diverse communication plan, even the best-laid goals for school improvement can fall flat.

Don't forget, you shouldn't do this work in isolation. Get your teams together to help create and implement the communication plan. You will be stronger together, and you will elevate your shared leadership. If you are new to school improvement, we encourage you to check out the work of Rick DuFour, Rebecca DuFour, Robert Marzano, John Hattie, Linda Darling-Hammond, Douglas Reeves, and Mike Schmoker, as they make up a powerhouse of school improvement experts, and their suggestions truly work to move the dial when it comes to advancing students.

My strength lies in implementation rather than the uncharted waters of innovation. Instead of dreaming up brand-new ways of teaching, I stay grounded with educational research in order to put best practices into action effectively. In my school, I chose to focus on three areas I felt would leverage student outcomes: (1) strengthening grade-level team collaboration, (2) implementing positive behavior supports, and (3) refining our system for academic interventions. I felt it in my core that if we strengthened the supports for all students, we would have less-intense needs in the top levels of our intervention tiers.

We canceled half of the staff meetings and replaced them with data team or professional learning communities (PLC) meetings. We deferred the wisdom of the team, agreed on ways to collaborate, and committed to systems like pacing calendars and assessments.

By amplifying the voices of the classroom and empowering teams to make collective decisions, we began strengthening differentiation and grade-level interventions.

To navigate changes in our positive behavior interventions and supports (PBIS) system, we hired an outside consultant. We needed to have hard conversations, and sometimes having a neutral facilitator helped us navigate those tender spots so we could move faster. We identified the mission of the group and strengthened the team through subcommittees. We set goals and created systems for recognizing positive behaviors. It shifted our culture to embracing a growth mindset, and it became a real bright spot in our building.

With the data teams and PBIS moving in the right direction, we were then able to look at our system for academic intervention. We were able to see the kids who were not making progress in the classroom and to use common data to put resources where they needed to go.

Within a year, these three initiatives helped to leverage our student achievement and shift outcomes for kids. We went from the bottom of our state in student growth to the top. When you focus on what research tells you works best and implement it well, the outcomes can be powerful.

KEEP FOCUSED

Think back to the chart in the previous chapter where you outlined the strongly and weakly aligned tasks you tackle on any given day. In order to "go deep," you're going to need to first identify with your staff those activities that don't serve your greater collective purpose. Educational researcher Doug Reeves talks in his work about "weeding the garden" before embarking on change. Meaning that, in our field, we often have too many initiatives and ideas overwhelming our priorities, and these push out the things we truly want to have and do. As leaders, we need to clarify our focus. Think of all of the demands on you and your staff. What can you stop doing? As you are pondering this, you might consider asking your team, "What gets in the way of your best work?"

There will no doubt be some low-hanging fruit in their responses. You might hear that they don't have time to make three positive phone calls home to parents per week, or that the meeting schedule leaves them without a day to collaborate as a team. Listen deeply so that when you choose an area of focus, you can say, "Okay folks, this isn't working. We are going to stop doing X to make room for Y, because Y is more important." You will only be able to do that when you understand your staff's perceptions.

The hardest part of deciding to go deep is maintaining your focus through the inevitable ups and downs. When things are going well, it's easy to get distracted by something new and shiny and think, Hmm, maybe we should do that instead? In dark and gloomy times, it's easy to say, "Grr, this is impossible! Let's forget it." Change doesn't happen overnight, and it certainly doesn't happen when you change course too often. There are so many talented yet misguided administrators who steer their team in circles because they don't commit to the long-term plan. Choose three focus areas. Choose them carefully. Execute them fully, well, and with purpose.

HOLD YOURSELF ACCOUNTABLE

Consider ways to hold yourself accountable to your goals. Use technology to help you think long-term. For example, maybe your August self sends your January self an email that says, "Hey, January is a great time to buckle down and focus on teacher clarity." Many email programs have ways to schedule delivery. Boomerang, an email extension, is one great tool that does this. Draft reflections for yourself about your initiatives and have them come to you via email throughout the year. Create a repeating event in your Google calendar to prompt yourself to reflect on your goals, with names such as "Are you giving feedback on precision partner talks?" In addition, make space in your weekly memos to staff to include your goals, or include them at the top of every staff meeting agenda. You might also think about incorporating your goals as part of your walkthrough tool, with observable actions listed below each goal.

Repetition is the key. At any point during the year, your staff should be able to spout off the school-wide goals.

One of the most prevalent ways principals lose focus is by getting mired in the demands of challenging student behavior. When principals focus their time and energy on 3 percent of students and their teachers, they create the conditions for the remaining 97 percent to stray from the initiatives that will leverage success. Focus instead on systems that will meet behavior needs. For example, solidify your behavior matrix for common areas around the school, clarify with your staff what is a classroom versus principal referral issue, or provide reinforcement to students who make positive choices. Just remember to trust your team and appreciate those who are responding first to incidents, but try not to put yourself at the center of every issue.

As leaders, we must realize we will never achieve optimal results if we are running from one incident to the next. When we are spending all our time responding to unsavory behavior, we are unable to focus on teaching and learning. Think about leveraging your existing staff to help support students by formulating a building-wide approach to create a positive culture. It is imperative that we shift our attention and efforts to support our marginalized students. Sometimes you might discover that the underlying cause of misbehavior is lack of engagement with teaching and learning.

We are very empathetic to the conundrum of time and student behavior. We can hear you saying, "Yeah right, that would be nice," "Yeah, but you don't know this kid," "I'm the only one that can . . . ," "My team needs me to . . . " Please know we are nodding and smiling with deep empathy. Understand if you are in this situation, you are not alone. Addressing students' behavior and mental health is something principals are dealing with coast to coast. Mental health is critically important and needs to be addressed, but we are suggesting that your job is to monitor how it is addressed, rather than trying to address it all by yourself, John Wayne style. You are not superhuman. You literally cannot be in more than one place at any one time, and so, you have to put yourself in the place where your impact will be the biggest, and that, friends, is in instructional leadership.

------------------------------- *Kate* -------------------------------

In recent years, there has been a palpable shift in how our students have entered our schools. There has been a noticeable decrease in students' academic readiness, but the most drastic change has been around behavior and emotional regulation. I have talented staff who spend hours planning brilliant lessons, and yet they never get the opportunity to teach them because student behavior paralyzes the entire classroom. Although we prided ourselves on having calculated behavior systems, our data was showing that we were really struggling with our earliest learners. We were spending an enormous amount of time *reacting* to dysregulation in the early grades, and our referral data showed it. We noticed our students were often coming to us disconnected from their peers and adults. They had no idea how to work with others and play in socially appropriate ways. They didn't know how to handle disappointment, take turns, or use coping skills to work through adversity. These young students were emotional. It was taking all our efforts to help them maintain, while their academics were put on the back burner. We spent literally entire days following students in the hallways or eventually sending students home. We had to do something before we eternally lost these students to suspensions, self-contained classrooms, and, in some cases, inevitable incarceration. We needed to find ways to bring our children closer to us instead of pushing them away.

We decided that it was vital to give children regulatory and social skills before they entered into the K–12 system. We needed a preschool that focused on helping our young children feel connected to and loved by their greater community. Our preschool needed to focus not on academics, but on social and emotional competency. Our preschool needed to grow empathetic students who celebrated differences and helped the overall cohesiveness of the classroom. We decided to go deep into a realm I knew very little about . . . social emotional intelligence in early childhood.

After I pleaded with him relentlessly, our superintendent approved my vision to start a preschool. I often tease that he agreed just to shut me up, when actually he was a champion for early childhood. We partnered with our county's early learning childhood program that services our birth-to-age-five children with disabilities. They were instrumental in providing funding, as well as resources, guidance, professional learning, and pep talks. In a few short months, our preschool took off. I felt like we were building the plane while we were flying it. I made too many mistakes to count. However, I had a profound commitment to the notion that we had to start teaching our precious children the social and regulation skills necessary to be successful in our K–12 world. We had a committed obligation to create a system of regulation and social connectedness that would not only be infused in preschool, but our entire PK–5 building.

In order to devote my energy to creating an early learning system, I set aside other initiatives and projects. I felt, at times, that I was letting people down. I would find myself being coaxed and pulled in other directions. However, I believed strongly that integrating a preschool into our existing system was irrefutably important. My efforts were calculated and focused on creating a program that would give children and staff the skills to connect and regulate.

Our commitment to go deep on this goal has paid off in more ways than I can articulate. In the last two years, we have decreased our behavior referrals at the kindergarten level from forty to six. Our students are visibly more empathetic and inclusive. In addition, we have dramatically decreased the number of students going into self-contained classrooms. Lo and behold, our academic achievement has increased, as well. In the last two years, we have had only two students who participated in our preschool not make benchmark status on our reading assessment at the end of kindergarten. In addition, we have received the highest rating on our English language state assessment. We can't wait to see, as the students rise through the grades, the

overall continued impact on social, behavioral, and academic achievement. Choosing to vigorously adopt this route has had a lasting impact
on our school culture, academic progress, and connectedness.

When you are clear on the vision for your school and know the
areas that will help you get there, the path will illuminate. Establishing
your goals helps you know when to say yes and when to say no. It clar-
ifies decisions on how to budget and where to put resources. When the
myriad of requests detonates unexpectedly, you can ask of each one,
"Does this fit with our focus? Does it help us move forward?" If the
answer is not a robust "Absolutely!" then put it aside for a different time.
Trust us, there will be time to address more areas when you have a year
or two of success under your belt. However, first things first: focus, dig
deep, and watch your students and staff soar.

INVITATION TO IMPLEMENT

- Focus and prioritize. Look at your data and identify three areas
  that will be your focus.
- Examine the competing areas on your plate and identify what
  is not in alignment with your focus. Make a list of what you and
  your staff could stop doing.
- Do some research on common teaching strategies that could
  be implemented throughout your building. Create a plan on
  how to teach, model, and reinforce these strategies throughout
  the year.
- Set up a time to establish or reestablish your teams.
  - Look at the questions we provided in this chapter and
    tweak them to meet your teams' needs.
  - Become familiar with having your teams create norms.

CHAPTER SIX

WORK THROUGH YOUR STRENGTHS

"Strong and cohesive teams thrive when leaders highlight how much they all have in common, not how much he or she stands above the crowd."

—Moira Alexander

*Y*our mouth gapes as you watch a talented colleague whip together a master schedule in the blink of an eye. A power struggle with a student evaporates as an associate saunters up, gives a simple direction, and the student dutifully follows, looking back at you with a smirk. A fellow leader spouts off about the hottest new social media app, while you try to figure out how to tag someone on Facebook. Tripping up the stairs, three minutes late to a 4:30 district office meeting with vomit spattered on your shoes, marker ink smudged up your arm, and your Spanks riding up your thigh, you encounter the perfectly coiffed colleague who looks like she just stepped off the runway. Do you feel like you're surrounded by leaders who seem to have it all figured out, while you are left staring at the little red alert box on your phone, taunting you with 279 unread emails?

Many leaders tumble into feelings of deficiency and spend more time focusing on their shortcomings rather than leaning into their strengths. And why not? It's easy to focus on the admirable traits other people possess, all the while questioning your own lack of proficiency. On our murkier days, the deep fog of envy, need for control, and perfectionism steals our ability to realize our strengths and fills us with self-doubt, insecurity, and inertia.

Given the amount of information pulsing from our devices at any given moment, it's hard not to get caught up by comparison. On a single Sunday afternoon, we can watch Principal Gerry Brooks humorously speak in his car about educational trends, read about energized leaders who turn around dismally performing schools in a single year, and learn of charismatic rock stars that can spark enthusiastic engagement with just one well-crafted phrase. The thought of sifting through mountains of data and coming up with an effective formula lands you in Snoozeville. While these inspirational people do provide us with ideas, hopes, and dreams, let's admit it: they can also make us feel inadequate.

Try as you might, emulating other incredible school leaders may not be easy or feel natural. It may not fit your true style. We've all longingly watched other educators and wished we could be like them, but time and time again, without authenticity, we fall short. Instead of creating a viral-worthy clip, we just end up in the ditch. So, what should we do about it? Kick that deficit mindset to the curb, is what you should do, and construct your own yellow brick road to strength-based leadership. Pause and focus on your own assets and talents. Blow away that oppressive fog, take a deep breath of fresh perspective, wipe the vomit off those shoes, and let's get busy highlighting what makes you the best you!

Strengths. You know, those assets that are part of your DNA, or skills you've acquired by working diligently. Strengths anchor you, make you feel invincible, and give you the confidence to take on the world.

There isn't a single human being that doesn't have strengths, and when you give full attention to yours, amazing transformation can take place. Author and researcher Tom Rath discovered that people have several times more potential for growth when they invest energy in developing their strengths, rather than correcting their deficiencies.

We adore acronyms in the education world, so we certainly did not want to disappoint. We've created one below to help you leverage your strengths. In doing so, you'll become more resilient, more productive, and put the *you* back into your own leadership style.

S: See
T: Target
R: Recognize
E: Enlist
N: Narrow
G: Gather
T: Transform
H: Heighten

See your strengths. Start by spending some time paying attention to all you have to offer to identify your strengths. Write down a strength and then tally each time you exemplify that strength. You may start right when you wake up by writing "self-care" on your list, because you got eight hours of sleep, ate a healthy breakfast, and meditated for fifteen minutes prior to hopping in the shower. That's three instances of this strength—and it isn't even 6:30 a.m. yet!

As you enter your building, instead of going through the front door, you come in through the multipurpose room, which houses your on-site daycare. You greet several adults, hug a few students, and check in with the custodian about an assembly that day. You haven't hung up your jacket yet, but you've already added "connector" to your list of strengths and exhibited it three times. As the coffee pot is brewing, you check that the handouts for the staff meeting are ready, create a folder on your desktop to hold downloaded teacher goal-setting documents, and consult your calendar and set up two reminder alarms on your phone to do observations later that day. Slap "organized" on your strengths list.

The students and their families are soon rushing through the doors. As the bells rings, you notice one of your assistants coming in late. This is the third time in the last two weeks this person has been tardy. The easy thing would be to let it slide and avoid conflict, but you document the incident and ask to meet with the employee after school. During that meeting you show your documentation, share the punctuality expectation, and inquire as to the reason behind the tardiness. Although it may have made you uncomfortable, you can add "accountability" to your list of strengths.

As your list grows, bask in the glow of all your talents. If you notice you're starting to compare yourself to influencers on social media, read that beautiful list of strengths again and be confident in your own abilities.

In addition to analyzing your day to create your own list of strengths, consider using an assessment tool. There are many out there, including Strengths Based Leadership, Myers-Briggs, and Enneagram, just to name a few. All of these surveys ask a variety of questions that will help you determine your strengths. You can also use these tools with your staff to get them thinking more about their own leadership style and strengths, and to help them see the strengths in others.

Target certain attributes and build upon them. We find it is much easier to build upon or tweak a strength we already possess than to start at a deficit with quality that does not come naturally to us. Now that you have your list, it is time to really home in on a few strengths that will leverage results. If you are a naturally effective communicator, go deeper with your communication, vary your audiences to include additional stakeholders, or learn a new way to communicate. For example, some of us are prolific emailers. In fact, there are those people (*ahem* . . . Kate) that actually need an intervention to stop overcommunicating via email. Since she loves interacting with her community, she might try utilizing social media, a new texting app, or Google Docs. She may also consider streamlining email by combining individual emails into one.

In my first principalship, I took the position vacated by one of my dear friends, who couldn't possibly be more different than me. He exuded charisma and energy in everything he did. His brain worked at warp speed, and he had every detail memorized. At recess, he played basketball with the boys and played Kidz Bop from his phone. He was fun, fun, fun.

I was also leaving a teaching position in a building where I worked with an award-winning principal. She had systems for the systems and an unwavering, laser-like focus. So much of her style made sense to me, but I had no idea how to build one like it myself.

In addition, I was lucky enough to be assigned a mentor whose wisdom and style were unique. She had central-office experience and a calm that comes from years of working in schools. She would ask questions that made me think she knew I was a hot mess, but that she wanted me to come to my own conclusion.

A big reason why my first season of being a principal was unsuccessful was because I was trying to take on the styles of other people. I was attempting to fill their shoes by wearing them. It didn't work. Things did not get better for me until a wise mentor who had known me for decades reminded me of something very important: If I wanted to be authentic, I needed to be me. I sat back and thought about the hard stuff I had done in the past and the ways I had brought about change on the teams I'd worked on. My strengths were in being thoughtful, understanding research, listening, and relating to others. I needed to give myself permission to disappoint some people by not being someone else.

Once I began leading from an authentic place, I started gaining traction. I found myself being able to laugh, relate, and connect. When I would share ideas, they were grounded in my own core beliefs. The thing is that people respond to authenticity; it can be felt and received.

R **Recognize** that your greatest strength can also be your most profound weakness. It is true, friends. Have you ever heard that too much of a good thing can be a problem? Be mindful of how your strengths can have drawbacks and impact others. Many of us are multitasking fiends! We can talk on the phone and sign purchase orders, all while giving a student a sensory break. While productivity is a fabulous strength, multitaskers may need to evaluate the quality of their work and check on how present they are when in the company of others.

Consider compassion and empathy: These are wonderful strengths, and just like any strength, these qualities come more naturally to some than others. However, compassion and empathy can creep into our personal lives and cause disruption. How many of us have lain awake at night worrying about a student, a family, or a member of our staff? We may have difficulty setting boundaries and become too involved with supporting people in our work world. Navigating these strengths is an art form, not a science. Remember, sometimes we are tested, not to necessarily show our weaknesses, but to discover our strengths.

> Remember, sometimes we are tested, not to necessarily show our weaknesses, but to discover our strengths.

E **Enlist** the people in your circle (mentors, staff, bosses, friends, family) to give you feedback on your perceived strengths. Your perception may not be everyone else's reality. According to Tom Rath, Gallup researchers studied more than one million work teams, conducted over twenty thousand in-depth conversations with leaders from various sectors, and polled more than ten thousand of his readers around the world to determine what attributes are associated with strong leadership. Researchers routinely encountered leaders who thought they were strong in particular areas, but their employees observed the complete opposite. We all have somewhat skewed views of ourselves. Therefore, seize the opportunity to get feedback on your strengths from a variety of stakeholders.

Think about all those speakers you've listened to at conferences and meetings. The majority must think they are engaging, charismatic and insightful. Why else would they be in the spotlight? You, on the other hand, might think they should be pulled off the stage with a cane. Wouldn't it be great if someone in their circle was able to give them feedback to help them improve?

You may be thinking, "Really? You want me to have my coworkers, friends, family, and complete strangers tell me if I'm strong in a certain area? Isn't that fishing for a compliment?" If you frame it the right way, by sharing that you want to improve your craft, you'll likely find people will be honored to give you feedback. For example, you might invite your boss to look for engagement during a staff meeting. After debriefing an observation with a teacher, ask if the feedback was useful and how you could have made it more valuable. Give a survey to parents with a series of questions that indicate if they find you approachable.

The other way is by being observant and self-aware. If you feel one of your strengths is managing time, but you go over by five minutes in every meeting, then that is a signal you may not be as strong in that area as you think. If you perceive you are an effective communicator, but your staff asks multiple clarifying questions *every* time, go back and evaluate the content of the communication and how you conveyed the message. If you regularly give presentations, watch for how often people check their phones, if they make eye contact, and whether they seem engaged. Sure, we can all have off days, but take note of patterns and reflect on why that pattern may be happening.

N **Narrow** your focus to work on yourself before you start working on others. This concept is true not only with our significant others, but in our work world, as well. It is easy to find faults with our colleagues and to blame failures on other people, systems, funding, parents, students, etc. There will be plenty of time to dissect *all* the reasons why something or someone is not successful, but we have to start with the person we have the most control over—ourself. If we are not confident in our strengths and abilities and aware of our weaknesses, how can we expect anyone else to embrace our leadership?

Start by making a web (see the example below). Put the current problem you're facing in the middle. Then, identify your strengths that relate to the problem and fill in one of these on each spoke. For example, if your problem is staff showing up late to meetings, and one of your strengths is not shying away from tough conversations, add that to a spoke on your web. Under each strength, write down how you can use that particular quality to mitigate the issue. If your strength is communicating your "why," note underneath that you can share in your staff meetings and in your handbooks the importance of being on time. Your web could have one spoke or five. The important thing is that you recognize your strengths and how you might apply them.

On the flip-side, if you are lacking depth in a particular strength, think about how you can use your resources to enhance that ability so you can more optimally solve your problems. For example, using the punctuality problem below, perhaps you are great with sharing your expectations, but not the best with following through consistently. Recognize and own that you may need some support. Technology can help! Add a reminder to your calendar to do certain tasks once a month. Perhaps you could create one to remind you to celebrate staff members who were on time, or to put up a flyer by the mailboxes with the start and end times of the upcoming staff meeting, or to communicate in your weekly bulletin why it is important to be on time. Another way to use your resources to help you develop a strength is to have an accountability partner to keep you on track. Perhaps you could encourage your professional learning teams to adopt punctuality as one of their norms, and to hold each other accountable for timeliness. That is called shared leadership!

Example: Focus Web

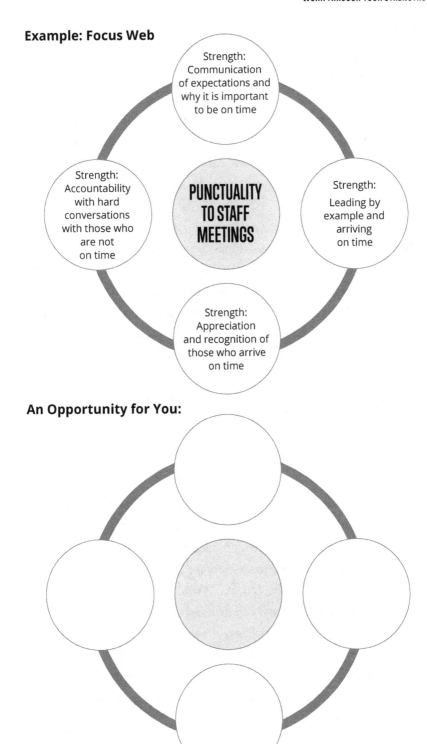

Strength:
Communication
of expectations and
why it is important
to be on time

Strength:
Accountability
with hard
conversations
with those who
are not
on time

**PUNCTUALITY
TO STAFF
MEETINGS**

Strength:
Leading by
example and
arriving
on time

Strength:
Appreciation
and recognition of
those who arrive
on time

An Opportunity for You:

G **Gather** people around you who complement your own strengths. Did you grow up with the notion that you needed to be well-rounded and involved in as many activities as possible? Were you involved with sports, student council, chess club, and drama all at the same time? Did you balance honor society with jazz band, all while competing on the speech team? It sure filled up your résumé, but it was exhausting, right? Many of us have carried this concept into our work lives. We want to do it all, and we want to do it all right now—and it is *still* exhausting.

Does being well-rounded make you an effective leader? According to Tom Rath, well-rounded individuals who tried to develop skills in all areas were actually mediocre leaders. Instead, effective leaders capitalize on their strengths and avoid being stretched too thin by taking on too much. Although there is a perception out there that some leaders "have it all," the fact is, they don't. What they do have is the ability to identify their personal strengths, recognize their weaknesses, and surround themselves with people who complement them and fill in the gaps. While the most effective leaders are not well-rounded, the best teams are diversified in their strengths.

Kate

One of my favorite times during the week is Monday mornings after all the students are settled in the classrooms. This is the time when I reserve thirty high-powered minutes for my leadership team to connect with each other to synchronize schedules, share when we might need to be off-walkie, talk about students and staff that might need support, and divide and conquer tasks and responsibilities. This dynamic group of educators is my dream team, and the awesome thing is that we are all very different. We love and respect each other deeply, but like any team, there are times when we may get on each other's nerves, miscommunicate, or straight up disagree, and most of the time I sit back and smile with pride.

We have a stronger community at Cherry Park Elementary *because* we disagree and challenge one another's thinking. Yes, it is sometimes uncomfortable, and it actually takes practice. However, overall, it adds thoughtful pause to our decision-making and depth to our understanding. Although my goal is to have our whole community moving in the same direction to meet shared goals at our school, this does not mean that we all go about it the same way or always agree with one another. Building a cohesive team that has varied strengths and perspectives all starts with hiring the right people.

I think one of a principal's most important jobs is hiring. I take great pride in the time, effort, and intentionality I place into getting the right people in the right positions. Several years ago, I had the opportunity to hire an academic coach. We had a very talented group of teacher-leaders with a diverse array of talents apply for the job. Although there were more logical choices, I took a risk and selected Miki. Miki was a high school counselor who had been out of the elementary grades for an extended period of time. She didn't know much about our current curriculum, assessments, or strategies, and yet, I hired her anyway. I hired her because she brought a perspective that I didn't have, and I knew she was a big-systems thinker. She is a whiz at master scheduling (not my area of expertise) and loves in-depth research (not my favorite). Miki is also relational to the core, and I knew that our veteran staff needed someone who was going to love first and push second. I, on the other hand, am a very detailed-oriented person who has checklists on every surface. I pride myself on data-driven decision-making, and on knowing effective strategies and how to supplement curriculum. I am doer, while Miki is a thinker. Although I consider myself very relational, I tend to plow ahead to get something done instead of taking a moment and thinking of the larger goal. Miki balances me and makes me pause to think about things differently. She is the first one who says, "Are you sure you want to send that email?" We respectfully disagree all the time, and it makes our community stronger.

T **Transform** your leadership capabilities one person at a time. We've all heard the saying "It is important to get the right people on the bus." What does that really mean, and why is it an important part of effective leadership? One of the first steps in developing a well-rounded team involves examining your hiring practices. When you are developing your pre-interview process—screening candidates, devising questions, and putting together your interview team—take that list of strengths you created for yourself and compare it to your existing team's strengths. Note what strengths are missing. Perhaps your team lacks technology integration expertise. Add a task to your interview process that measures skill in this area. Perhaps you want a warm and inviting office area, but don't have a decorator bone in your body. Although not a typical interview question, perhaps that is something you could glean by asking the candidates their hobbies or strengths. Look at your staff composite and compare it with your demographic data. Do your staff demographics reflect your student population? Do you have equal gender representation in your science department? Do you have a tendency to hire people only from a certain college or who have particular personality traits, like being humorous, outspoken, or compliant?

The key is to be strategic in determining who can complement your leadership qualities. In each seat of that bus is an important part of your community. With you as the driver, filling those seats with a variety of talents and strengths will move you all down the road toward your collective goals.

Rachael

When I needed to make my first hire as a building principal for the office manager who also served as my secretary, one of our school's most vital positions, I was reminded of a mentor's words: "Know your strengths and surround yourself with those who complement your weaknesses." As I worked my way through the applications, I kept an eye out for those who would bring skills to the table that I didn't have, like working with a budget. Sure, I had taken a school budgeting class in college, but actually managing a $300,000 budget felt a little bit intimidating. Near the end of the pile of applications, I found what I was looking for: a candidate who had extensive budgeting and purchasing experience at the county and city level. This was my gal!

After conducting a full day of interviews, including the candidate with budgeting experience, I was sold that this was the right person for the job and for me. My supervisor, however, didn't quite agree. She felt we needed someone with a different demeanor and personality than the candidate I had my eye on. After much debate, I was able to hire my first pick, and she ended up being the best fit. I was able to help teach her about customer service and schools, while she was able to run the books and manage the technical work behind the scenes. I periodically reflect on this first hire. If I had listened to my supervisor, I would have gone with another candidate, rather than someone who complemented my weaknesses. Looking back, I am so thankful that I came at this position from a strengths-based approach, as it truly made the difference in moving the building and school forward.

Heighten your creativity and productivity by surrounding yourself with people *unlike* yourself. Some may say it is easier to lead people who are like you, but this may not push you or your community to grow. If you are someone who is a big-picture thinker but allows the details to go by the wayside, make sure you have someone on your team who thrives on detailed work. You may possess the "get 'er done" gene; if so, make sure you have someone in your arsenal who can say, "Chill out, our staff is not on the same freight train as you, and they need more processing time." Developing a team with varied strengths doesn't just happen. It takes thoughtful and conscientious decision-making. There is a saying: "If you want to go quickly, go alone. If you want to go far, go together." We used to think it was an indictment of the solitary runner who wanted to go quickly, until we realized that speed and distance are morally neutral objectives. There are times when we need to go fast, and there are times when we need to go far. Some people need to do one more often than the other. Remember a diverse teams brings power to your work, so lean into your strengths.

INVITATION TO IMPLEMENT

- Reflect. Identify your top strengths to give you a mental image (and boost your confidence). One fun way to do this is with both words and with pictures. Start by making a list of your strengths. Then search for images and hunt through your own files to find a picture that matches the word. This is a great activity that can be just for you, or you may consider sharing it with your leadership group or staff.

- Make your system well-rounded, rather than striving to be well-rounded yourself. Brainstorm ways you can surround yourself with people who complement your weaknesses. Encourage your team to take the StrengthsFinder test, then evaluate which strengths are prevalent and which ones are missing. Have a discussion on how to capitalize on strengths, identify the gaps, and recruit someone with attributes that enhance the overall team's performance.

-PART THREE-

CONNECT

CHAPTER SEVEN

KNOW YOUR PEOPLE AND NAVIGATE PERSONALITIES

"There's no key to great relationships, there's
simply a well-worn welcome mat."

—Curtis Tyrone Jones

*Y*ou are about to hit send on an email to the entire staff, and you know it is going to trigger some uncomfortable feelings with at least a few of them. You worry about being misunderstood. It is important to get this information out promptly, but you contemplate if email is the best way to communicate. Although efficient, you worry people won't glean your intonation, even with all those emojis. So, you decide to shift your communication plan and wonder if you should call an emergency staff meeting at the end of the day. This way you could see their reactions, and they could feel your vibe. Although there would be guaranteed scowls and arms folded across chests, maybe it would be worth the risk. Nope . . . you decide against it. If people hear the words "emergency meeting," they always imagine the worse possible scenario.

They are already up to their eyeballs in stress and on the verge of imploding as it is, so you'd better avoid adding to the heap. Would a memo in their mailboxes accompanied by a Hersey's Kiss have more of a soft touch? You shake your head. Then, everyone hears the information at a different time and the rumor mill explodes. Plus, Harold is allergic to chocolate. Although inefficient, perhaps you could clear your afternoon schedule to share the news in person with as many professional learning teams as possible. Maybe if you just pushed that other project aside, you could make it happen.

Aaaah! The internal struggle is real, friends. Every day we have many choices to make, various personalities to consider, and unpredictable reactions to anticipate. It is a complicated world to navigate, and it takes practice. Let's dive in and learn strategies and techniques to use with the various personalities and their undoubtedly diverse reactions in your building.

Most of us enter this profession to make a difference. It isn't merely a job, but a quest to make an impact. We don't look at our jobs merely as occupations, but rather as *occupassions*. We're passionate about teaching those first sounds of the alphabet that ultimately lead students to graduation day, as "Pomp

> It isn't merely a job, but a quest to make an impact.

and Circumstance" filters through the auditorium. We're passionate about coaching struggling teachers who are ready to leave the profession to help them reach exemplary status on the evaluation rubric. We're passionate about encouraging our families to not merely be bystanders, but active participants in their child's education. We're passionate about collaboration and finding synergy with our fellow leaders, so that we can collectively share the burdens and the celebrations of our chosen work. Let's face it: We are in the people profession. Whether those people are five or fifty-five, ultimately our greatest passion is connecting with others to facilitate learning, generate positive change, and make our world a better place.

KNOW YOUR STAFF

Although our greatest delight may be working with people, one of the most challenging parts of our chosen profession is—you guessed it—the people. Depending on your situation, you could be interacting with hundreds, if not thousands, of people per day. That means negotiating a massive number of personalities, opinions, and feelings. Although it can be utterly exhausting, it is critically important to creating a cohesive community.

Navigating personalities starts with the lesson that giving and receiving verbal and nonverbal communication is an art. As author and former presidential speech writer James Humes wrote, "The art of communication is the language of leadership." We must become translators of sorts, skilled at predicting behavior and understanding triggers for glee, sorrow, excitement, and frustration. We must understand the meaning behind mood swings, disengaged blank stares, and midnight emails from parents, staff, or students. There are many of us who also add a multitude of cultures and languages to our interpretive practice. We must learn to ask questions, clarify nonverbal communication, and decipher events. Doing this well takes dedication, practice, and perseverance.

A leader's most potent superpower is knowing their people. Doing so develops deliberate connections over time, transitions casual affiliations to meaningful relationships, and leads to significant growth and development. Take a moment and brainstorm the ways you purposefully get to know the people in your sphere:

1.
2.
3.
4.

Remember, we all have different styles and need to do what is comfortable for both ourselves and the people we are getting to know. Although a team-building weekend retreat may be ideal for some people, you can get the same results by spending a little extra time popping by classrooms to shoot the breeze in the morning, or by making a point of sitting next to someone you don't know well at a meeting. As you plan your staff meetings, think about incorporating purposeful activities that build trust and connection prior to jumping into the business part of the agenda.

Everyone brings their personality with them to work. While behaviors can change and skills can be learned, personality tends to remain constant. Personality traits are like preferences for the ways people interact with others, take in information, make decisions, and organize their lives. Skills that lie outside of these personality-based preferences can be learned, for example, a shy, reserved person can learn the skills to be a gregarious presenter in front of a classroom, but chances are their preference will always be for quieter interactions. The goal is not to change the personalities of others, or label one personality preferable over others. Recognizing and appreciating the variety of personalities on your team helps you understand how best to work together to amplify your impact on students.

> Recognizing and appreciating the variety of personalities on your team helps you understand how best to work together to amplify your impact on students.

Kourtney

Personality-wise, I am a big-picture person, 100 percent. Details tend to annoy me, and I frequently get them wrong. (Honestly, what's the difference between 6:00 p.m. and 6:30 p.m.? Answer: A lot when you get it wrong in a newsletter!) I am most inspired when I have the opportunity to dream about systems, possibilities, and making the world a more efficient place. I also tend to make decisions from a place of logic, making the choice to do the thing that is right, whether or not it makes people upset. This is both a blessing and a curse, let me tell you!

When I invited my team to do an ice breaker using some Myers Briggs–like prompts, we learned *a lot* about each other. When I asked them to divide themselves up into big-picture versus fine-detail-oriented people, 80 percent of the staff put themselves in the fine details camp. The majority of the team, I realized, saw the world from a very different perspective than I did.

It is truly important to recognize that personalities are not bad or good. We could still share a common vision, set goals together, and make change, but in order to do it, I needed to present information in a way that suited their personalities. For example, I once proposed a change to our master schedule, and learned that a fair number of people on my team preferred to make decisions based on the impact those decisions would have on others. I realized they wanted to understand the human side of change before jumping on board. This led me to pause and tell the stories of our kids who were not getting the interventions they needed because of the limitations of our master schedule. When my team saw the reasoning behind the proposal and connected to it emotionally, they understood the schedule change was necessary.

We all occasionally get distracted by the full range of personalities on display in our workplace. One derogatory comment at a staff meeting or one degrading comment on Facebook can propel leaders into a tailspin and make them lose focus. We all have a sensitively meter, and when navigating personalities, this meter can be your best friend or worst enemy. Being attuned to others' moods, words, and feelings can be a beautiful strength. Harnessed effectively, this kind of sensitivity can lead to curiosity, compassion, and informed decision-making.

Being sensibly empathetic can open doors to connection and differentiation. It allows you to receive transparent stimuli to make informed decisions. However, being overly sensitive is like having a weight tied to your ankle in a vast ocean, pulling you down to the darkest depths. Our feelings of inadequacy and the demons of despair can shatter our confidence and plunge our poised presence. On any given day, the dial on our sensitivity meter can vacillate, which makes it critical to know the power of sensitivity so you can regulate accordingly.

How many times have you heard the saying "You need a thick skin in this profession"? "Thick skin" insinuates that we won't let the actions of others penetrate our hearts and our minds. But do we really want skin so thick that we deflect connection with the very people who can give us valuable feedback to make critical decisions? We can react more thoughtfully and less emotionally if we are prepared to anticipate different personalities. As you are traversing the multitude of dispositions in your day-to-day, don't forget that all behavior has a function. As leaders, it is important to know the "why" behind the behavior. The more deeply you know your people, the better you'll come to understand and ultimately react to them. In addition, just like our students, the more we identify the "why," the less personal the behavior becomes. A staff member's outburst at a public meeting may suggest they are mad about a decision you made, when, in fact, the staff member may be feeling insecure and simply needs more professional development in a particular area. A person that passes you in the hallway without making eye contact or offering a greeting may not be avoiding you; perhaps their mind is elsewhere because they were up four times with a sick baby. Remember:

Before you assume, learn the facts.
Before you judge, understand why.
Before you hurt someone, feel.
Before you speak, think.

————————————————— Rachael —————————————

Regardless of what building I have been in as a teacher or administrator, we have had new staff join our school family. As each new staff member has come on board, our dynamics and the way we communicate have changed. We've tweaked the way feedback was provided, as new folks and younger folks prefer it to be communicated in a different way. When it came to knowing my people and how to interact with their personalities, things would change, sometimes unexpectedly.

These were hard lessons for me as a principal. I took people at face value and often didn't look to understand the deeper meaning behind their actions, inactions, or responses. Call me naive, but if they said something to me, I took it for what it was and assumed they were being transparent, all without realizing there was so much more below the surface.

Case in point, during my first few years as a principal, I provided feedback on an observation to a new teacher. I did so with a direct, clear, and coaching approach, which was consistent with what we had previously talked about as a team in the interview, as a staff during in-service, and during the first few months of the school year. It wasn't until I got to the part of the debrief that included tweaks or things to think about that I noticed their body language change. At the time, I wasn't sure what was behind it, but later, when they had avoided me for a bit, I knew we needed to talk.

As we sat down to check in, the teacher started crying hysterically. They shared that when I asked reflective questions about their practice, they weren't sure how to respond, because they just didn't know. Instead of taking this at face value, I opted to lean in to better understand. It turned out this new teacher needed more guidance and structure when it came to creating the ideal learning environment in their classroom, and my open-ended, reflective questions were not the best fit for where they were at in their journey.

This conversation led to a lot of reflection on my part. I felt terrible this new teacher felt bad and had had this experience with feedback. I wanted teachers to feel empowered, not full of self-doubt. In the end, I was worried I had harmed them for years to come, and that I wasn't as nimble of a leader as I needed to be. This experience made me realize that people have unique personalities, and communication styles can vary greatly. Here's to being intentional about getting to know your people and their personality types!

KNOW YOUR STUDENTS

Knowing your people includes not only your staff, but also your students. Just like the adults at our worksites, our children all have a story, as well. They have joys, and frustrations, and talents, and struggles. It is your job as a leader to truly know each student so you will be able to differentiate your interactions and tailor experiences for optimal growth. We believe that knowing your students is the first step in helping them grow, so get off the sideline and jump into their worlds.

We know this seems obvious, but start with learning and pronouncing their names correctly. There is significant power in using someone's name in a greeting. You can see it in the twinkle in their eyes and the way they stand up just a little straighter. Parents will grin from ear to ear if you recognize their child by name. It means their child is someone you care enough about to learn it. If remembering several hundred names feels overwhelming, try associating a student's name with something that describes them or that they are interested in that starts with the same letter. For example: Fernando Freckles, Solice Soccer, or Halima Haircut. Go up and down the lunch line practicing each person's name over and over again. You could also invite students to ask you "What is my name?" when you pass by. If you miss it, they get a point. Names are not only a powerful reinforcer but the best management tool and relationship enhancer there is. However you do it, take the time to imprint students' names in your brain.

KNOWING STUDENTS AS LEARNERS

The next step after learning your students' names is knowing them as learners. If we are destined to be instructional leaders who hold the power to create systems, structures, schedules, and personnel distribution, it is critical to know the many aspects and traits of your students. Not knowing can lead to blind decision-making. If you are new to your building, this may seem like a daunting task. However, this is a guaranteed winning strategy that will elevate your practice and lead to positive results. If you want to become knowledgeable about your students' skills, attend your building's data, behavior, and intervention meetings. There is nothing more important. The decisions made at these meetings move the dial for our students, which makes them a critical part of our work. Remember, you don't necessarily need to be the leader in charge of these meetings, but you certainly need to be part of the decision-making. In fact, this is a great way to build shared leadership; but to do so well, you must preplan with your leaders and sit at the table when these important conversations take place. Below are a handful of critical elements to enhance your knowledge of our learners so we can optimally serve them to their fullest potential. Consider how you know your students when it comes to academics, attendance, behavior, and families.

Academics: Strive to be a data geek and drill down to the student level. Commit time and effort to attend professional learning communities, data team meetings, and planning sessions. Be an integral part of your student intervention teams. If you know your students' academic strengths and weaknesses, you'll be able to strategically provide opportunities, assign personnel, shift schedules, and buy materials. Offer to progress monitor students, or cover a small group to deepen your knowledge of your students as learners. Twenty minutes of teaching first-grade reading or eleventh-grade chemistry can be insightful. Use this information to support not only the students in your school, but also your staff.

Attendance: If they aren't at school, we can't teach them, so investigate the why behind the absenteeism. Set your attendance expectations high and establish a concrete protocol for follow through. There is much speculation as to why students don't come to school, but the number one reason across all grade levels is the lack of a positive connection with an adult at the school. Make it a goal to be that one person who students come to school to see and/or cultivate a posse of people who will provide that connection. You can facilitate these student connections by speaking directly to the student or even by giving a survey asking who they feel connected with at school, and what specifically this adult is doing to make them feel included, cherished, and important. Analyze the list of traits that help kids connect for commonalities and trends. Then share it with your staff to expand and replicate.

Behavior: Behavior is undoubtedly our biggest time suck. We could have a perfectly planned day, only to be wiped out by a single student making unsavory choices. It is easy to become drained, frustrated, and defeated. The most effective behavior management tool is a meaningful relationship. Alfred Adler, an Austrian medical doctor who researched personality development, concluded that if a person feels valued, significant, and competent, they will generally act in a connected and cooperative way. Makes sense, right? Think about which people you like to be around and why. We bet they are people who make you feel accepted, appreciated, and important. We will generally work harder and put more effort in for those we like and who we know like us. It is no different with kids. You can proactively bring students closer to you by inviting them to lunch, shooting some hoops, or going to one of their sporting events or dance recitals. Get to know them and make them feel special. We must stop pushing our students away by suspending them and placing them in detention or timeouts. By focusing on positive relationships, the walls of defensiveness and anger will dissipate the more you come know and understand the people in your care.

Families: Leveraging family relationships is a power move. For decades, well intentioned educators have overlooked this asset and have instead viewed families with a deficit lens, noticing only the obstacles they bring to education. This is a big problem. We need to shift our thinking to recognize the incredible gift families are to our students, and that every family wants their child to be successful. We only have our students with us for 35 out of the 168 hours in their week. Although we can make a powerful impact in those 35 hours, to truly understand and support them, we need to learn from and get to know their families. Families set the weather at home for how our students feel about school.

The parent who feels slighted, snubbed, and silenced by school will weave that narrative through interactions with their student at home. When their child communicates a frustration about an assignment, it will be amplified by the negative feelings that were planted by a lack of partnership. Alternatively, a family that feels supported, heard, and welcome will communicate those positive feelings about school in their interactions with their child. Our parents have a lot to offer, so take the time to get to know them and involve them in decision-making. Instead of talking *at* them during conferences, spend time asking them questions:

> **Families set the weather at home for how our students feel about school.**

- How is your student liking school?
- What does homework look like for your child?
- Does your child feel connected to friends?
- What do you need from us to help your child feel more successful?

By seeking to understand their experience with the school, you will be able to meet them where they are and truly partner with them. Conferences are not about educators disseminating information, but rather a conversation where we learn from one another. Establish some flex time with your staff and incorporate home visits throughout the year. The amount of information you can glean from a fifteen-minute visit in a child's home is invaluable and communicates deep caring for the family as a whole. It is as important to create a bond with your students' family members as it is with your students themselves.

Kate

There is so much joy and richness to be found when you go beyond the surface and learn someone's story. It not only brings you closer to that person, but can help you optimize how you navigate the people you interact with on a daily basis. One way we become enlightened at Cherry Park Elementary is by an activity called "Student Story."

We encourage all our staff to focus on two students per week and spend a few minutes asking them questions that give insights into their world. We then ask one staff member to present a student's story at the beginning of each staff meeting. The sharing begins by flashing the student's picture on the screen. Every time I look out, the staff members are grinning with anticipation. Teachers spend two minutes sharing the student's story, which may include the student's hopes and dreams, family traditions, or favorite food. Often, teachers will share what the child finds difficult, or their favorite things to do. Although we have a guide that includes questions staff can use when talking to a student, our hope is that a fluid conversation will take place.

Each time a staff member speaks of a student, we all learn something new. My favorite examples are when a staff member shares illuminating details about a misunderstood child. For example, a new student arrived at our school and was always incredibly loud. Staff would say, "Why does he have to be so loud?" His teacher chose this new student for a staff meeting story and explained that he had hearing loss and couldn't hear how loud he was speaking. You could see the lightbulb come on for many of us, and you can guarantee we switched our mindset from viewing him as an obnoxiously loud child who grated on our nerves, to one who needed empathy, understanding, and guidance to help with a disability. Without hearing his story, many of us would have never known and would have continued to misjudge him.

Although not as formal, I try every week to get to know parents on a deeper level. It is amazing how much you can learn by going out a few minutes before the bell rings and hanging out in the pickup area, or weaving in between the cars in the carpool lane to have brief conversations through the window. These extra few minutes of smiles, connections, and chatting pay off. By going below the surface, we gain a deeper understanding and create closeness. As we sink into their world, an intertwined bond forms that helps us navigate the personalities of both our students and their families.

KNOW YOURSELF

A critical piece to knowing the people in your community originates with knowing yourself. Aristotle said, "Knowing yourself is the beginning of all wisdom." We evolve each day through the experiences and people we encounter. Showing vulnerability and being open to knowing yourself a little better will lead to enlightenment. Ask yourself how your past experiences impact your ability to lead. Connecting the dots from your own story to your priorities and leadership style can give you tremendous insight.

As three white women who came from middle class backgrounds, we understand and know that our childhood and life experiences may be different than those of many others. We realize that white privilege played a role in developing who we are, and that many of our students and staff have very different life circumstances. As leaders, we have to constantly keep our bias and privilege in check as we get to know our students, staff, and families. Together as leaders, we need to grow our understanding of systemic racism and the impacts it has within our educational systems and how it affects those we serve. We encourage you to begin by listening to what your students, staff, and families need. They will tell you. As a team, examine how your systems and structures facilitate access and lend support, rather than working to uphold the barriers you seek to remove. Remember, we need to see and honor the color and culture of every family, all while being allies for them as we battle systemic racism in our world.

Spend some time answering the following questions: How has your past shaped your strengths and hindered your growth? How have your perspectives, values, and views changed over time as you've experienced shifts in roles, populations, or feedback? Have you looked deep into your biases or examined your privilege? These deep reflections will result in understanding yourself better so you can grow as a leader. Be aware there may be days when it is too painful to recognize what the signs are telling you. Other days, we may be braver and ready to embrace our reality. Most of us are our own worst critics, so be mindful of being kind to yourself. If you've made mistakes, join the club! Give yourself grace and continue to learn and evolve. In order for people to follow you, you must be confident in your wisdom and believe in yourself. Confidence will show itself when you understand yourself.

Example: Trait Analysis Chart

Event	Personality Trait	Why	Impact
Death of a parent at a young age	Controlling	I didn't have control over Mom's illness and ultimate death.	I need to be cognizant of micromanaging my staff.
Received a collegiate scholarship for soccer	Competitive/ driven	In order to be successful, I always need to be competitive.	I don't always need to be the best. I may need to work on my collaboration skills.
Moved 7 times in the first 5 years of schooling	Don't bond deeply	Each time I connected with someone, we moved, and it hurt.	I may put up a shield and not let my community get to know me.

An Opportunity for You

Event	Personality Trait	Why	Impact

INVITATION TO IMPLEMENT

- Make a list of significant events in your life. They can be from your childhood, adolescence, or something that occurred just last year.
- After you have created this list, write down how each event translates to certain traits in your personality, and why.
- Then link the personality trait to something in your work world. Start small with just one trait to see how you can either amplify it or tone it down.

CHAPTER EIGHT

EMBRACE HARD CONVERSATIONS

"Lean into the discomfort of the work."

–Brené Brown

*T*he bell has rung, and students are in their classrooms. The day has started, and students are settled into their seats. In our world, this time of day is perhaps the best part, as it holds so much potential for learning. As you start walking around the building, completing your morning check-ins with staff and students, you walk by a classroom where you overhear and view a staff member using a harsh and disrespectful tone with a student, while twenty-five pairs of eyes are staring at the berated student. Your euphoric mood has burst. As you cringe, you wonder if you should pop into the classroom to investigate. Perhaps you think, I don't want to embarrass anyone. I'll just pretend like I didn't hear it and move on down the hall to the classroom where I know they'll be excited and happy. Then you reconsider and decide, no, that is not the right thing. As uncomfortable as it is, it is time to do the essential work and plan for what could be a difficult conversation.

As a leader, people sometimes see you as the position rather than as a human. One of the hardest roles in the principalship is to act as a witness to the humanity of others. You are there on their best days, and you are there on their worst. There are times you see staff members accomplish heroic things, and times when you watch them make dreadful mistakes. You celebrate with families, and you observe some of their most challenging moments. It's not uncommon to be the recipient of harsh words, anger, and threats that under no other circumstances in your personal life would you allow to happen to yourself or others. Growing a thicker skin isn't the answer. As soon as you feel yourself doing that, it's time to invest in some serious self-care. The leader who leads with authenticity embraces the hard conversations, seeks to find commonalities, and above all, recognizes and respects people.

Rachael

"When you signed your contract, you agreed to do the hard work." These wise words by a mentor of mine often float through my brain when I am faced with a challenging conversation with a staff member, student, or family. As a leader, you didn't just sign up for the good parts of the job, you also signed up for the difficult parts. Like it or not, this includes having tough conversations with others.

Over the years, there have been a lot of these conversations. One of the most challenging ones was when I had to deliver the news to one of my teachers that her husband had passed away. There are many days that I reflect on this conversation and wish it had never happened. However, there was no way around it. As a leader, I had to think about how the conversation was going to be framed, how this was going to impact her, and what she was going to need personally and professionally. I also considered how I would want this situation to look and feel if it had been me receiving this information.

Before delivering the news, I briefed the office staff about what had happened and how we were going to respond. I then went to find her teaching partner and updated him on what had happened and next steps. She was really close to her teaching partner, so I had both classes covered and brought both of them down to the office. It was there that I sat next to her and shared the news I had just been told by the state police. Fortunately, the police were still on site and were able to provide her with additional details as we comforted her and held her hand. It was agonizing to see someone's life change before your eyes. My soul ached as I shared the news with her and realized that the discomfort I was feeling was nothing compared to what she was going through.

No matter how you look at these moments, these conversations, regardless of the topic, are hard. It hurts and strains our heart as we show empathy to the other person and their situation. Conversations like these stay with you, and the other person, for a lifetime. As you reflect back on them, you hope and pray that you show enough care for the other person involved, as there was no way around having them. Over time, I have realized that hard things happen and hard conversations are needed, but you don't have to be "hard" in how you go about delivering the news. I believe that being caring, compassionate, and understanding is all that matters.

Why should we have hard conversations? They're uncomfortable and awkward. No wonder we dread them. You might have even developed strategies to avoid them, like scurrying to your office to hide behind that lush fern on your desk each time a particular parent walks up the sidewalk. You may be guilty of paying your office assistant in Starbucks cards to screen calls or, knowing a certain staff member will seek you out after school, "suddenly" need to check if all the basketballs are properly inflated in the gym closet.

But avoiding hard conversations won't make the necessity for them disappear. In fact, you may be doing your students and staff a serious disservice by putting them off. In our career, we will undoubtedly *all* make poor hiring decisions or inherit incompetent staff. Even the best leaders will misread an interview or miscalculate the fit of a candidate. At some point, we will be transferred to a building where the previous leader just didn't have the time, energy, gumption, coaching ability, etc. to deal with a particular staff member. Although inevitable, the difference between successful and mediocre leaders is that the effective leader will acknowledge their mistake (or their circumstance) and step up to have the difficult conversation. Some of these challenging dialogues can lead to beautiful coaching and transformational change. Others can, and should, lead to a staff member's resignation or termination. Although these conversations are time-consuming and take preparation and concerted collaboration with your district leadership and union representation, in the long run, they will ultimately save leaders, staff members, and students a lot of heartache.

According to a 2018 article in *Education Week*, 44 percent of teachers leave within their first five years in the profession, costing districts thousands in hiring and training expenses to replace them. The top reasons teachers leave a particular building or the profession all together is that they are not getting enough support and don't feel connected to their community. Remember: hard conversations not only benefit the leader, but also the employee. Direct dialogue leads to transparency, which leads to support, which leads to more content staff, which leads to retention. It is extremely difficult to get traction on school improvement efforts if a leader has a constant turnover.

Leaders aren't the only ones who observe poor management, disorganized lessons, or unprofessional behavior. Fellow staff and community members notice, too. If you say that staff meetings begin at 8:00 a.m., and yet staff members are still trickling in at 8:15, with no accountability, what message does that send to your staff who arrive on time? Think of how many times you've sat in meetings where people have been plunking away on their computers or phones while a presentation was taking place. If the leader doesn't preserve standards of engagement, the audience will continue to bust through the established norms (if any were established), and resentment from others will grow. Lovingly keeping your community committed to high standards develops a positive culture that people want to be a part of. So, toss back some Tums and invest in your people by having the hard conversations. Some of our favorite books on this topic are *Hard Conversations Unpacked* by Jennifer Abrams, *Crucial Accountability* by Kerry Patterson et al., and *Fierce Conversations* by Susan Scott.

Working in education can be challenging, and the longer you're in your role as a school leader, the more you'll learn that different personalities produce different reactions to stress and fatigue. To help you prepare for the hard conversations you'll inevitably have, we'd like to introduce you to the "six Ds": dejected, defensive, delighted, dismissive, disengaged, and derogatory. We'll explore how these types of reactions might manifest in your setting, how to acknowledge and react to each behavior, and how you might start a conversation to gain understanding so you can respond appropriately.

Dejected

Looks like

- "I have been working twelve-hour days, and the students' data is horrible!" (as tears roll down their face).
- "I wasn't selected for the department chair AGAIN, and I've done everything you told me to do."
- "I am not available to help my child with their homework because I am working two jobs. I feel so guilty and ashamed."

Acknowledge/coach

- Recognize their work ethic and help them find glimmers of hope.
- Identify and develop their strengths through opportunities.
- Don't be afraid to have an honest conversation. Sometimes ripping off the Band-Aid hurts at the time, but is better in the long run.
- Reassure the parent that you know they are doing their best. Offer other resources that could help their child with homework. Remember, assume the best intent and don't make judgements.

Conversation starters

- The last time I observed I saw [specific praise]. How could you enhance this strategy?

- Let's find a student who has made some growth and identify the direct causes for their achievement . . .
- I understand you are disappointed. Have you considered developing your skills by . . .
- I appreciate that you are reaching out to support your child. We have an after-school club that has peer tutoring to help students with homework. Could I help you sign up your child? If that doesn't work for your schedule, I'd love to provide some online resources, like Khan Academy, that do a great job of explaining concepts.

Defensive

Looks like

- "I can't be responsible for teaching all those standards."
- "I can't believe those sixth-grade teachers didn't teach these students algebra. Now, our students are way too behind to take on our curriculum."
- "I had a room full of students with summer birthdays. That is why my data is so low."
- "I refuse to have the reading coach in my classroom. He tried to correct me on something I have been teaching just fine for the past twenty-five years."
- "I think I'll just write this email and send it to the curriculum director, telling her how lousy these assessments align with the curriculum."

Acknowledge/coach

- Acknowledge that they seem uncomfortable.
- Ask questions about their interpretation of the situation.
- Provide a third point of reference that makes the conversation more tangible and less confrontational, like data statements, an agenda, or a checklist, so that the focus is on the artifact, and not on you.

Conversation starters

- How are you feeling right now?
- I understand your point of view. May I suggest . . .
- Remember that the purpose of any data is to lead us to ask more questions. What questions do you have about this data?

Delighted

Remember, working with people isn't all negative!

Looks like

- "I like that you come into my classroom and give me suggestions on how to engage my students at a higher level."
- "I would really enjoy the leadership opportunity to chair our equity committee."
- "I am wondering if I could take a risk and try flexible and variable seating instead of desks in rows this year."
- "I really enjoyed our professional learning today around how to use Google Classroom, but the presenter went a little fast. Do you think you could share the PowerPoint with me?
- I think I really bombed that lesson, but I am looking forward to visiting the other teacher in our building to get ideas.

Acknowledge/coach

- Give opportunities for shared leadership experiences
- Depending on how best they like to receive acknowledgments, thank them in a weekly bulletin, write a personal note, or send a letter to their mom (remember adults have parents with refrigerators, too!).
- Get their opinions, use their ideas, and learn alongside them.

Conversation starters

- I see so much leadership potential in you. I was wondering if I could tap you for . . .

- Our school district has been asked to do a presentation at the state conference. Would you be interested in sharing how you implemented _____?
- I noticed how you were using some new strategies to give your students feedback. Would you show me what you are doing so we can share these ideas with others?

Dismissive

Looks like

- "I don't believe in this assessment. It is comparing apples to oranges. It doesn't represent what my students know."
- "I think this initiative is just another flavor of the month. I'll just wait it out until it goes away."
- They are nodding and smiling, but when they get back to their room, you know they'll do their own thing.
- "I get all my curricula from Teachers Pay Teachers. Feel free to take the shrink-wrapped district-adopted curriculum from the back shelf."

Acknowledge/coach

- Thanks for sharing your thoughts on the assessment. You are correct that this test isn't the end-all-be-all, but it is a normed, research-based assessment.
- I know that change is hard. Tell me how you are feeling about . . .
- Tell me when a good time would be to pop into your room to see . . .
- Let's look through this curriculum guide together and see what might fit into your lesson.

Conversation starters

- What other data did you bring that may show differing results?
- What information can we glean from this data to move forward?

- What knowledge could you contribute to strengthening this new idea?
- You have so much to offer this community. How can we work together to get this off the ground?

Disengaged

Looks like

- Their hood is up, their body is not facing the speaker, and they are not making eye contact.
- They scheduled a dentist appointment (again) on your professional development day.
- "I missed the deadline to turn in my survey. I just keep forgetting."
- I have nothing to offer the conversation, so I'll just check email from my phone.
- I think I'll tell my tablemates about this awesome deal I got on Amazon. The boss won't notice I'm having a side conversation. during his presentation.
- I think I'll correct papers during a staff meeting since this topic really isn't of interest to me.

Acknowledge/coach

- Acknowledge that they have many insights to bring to the conversation.
- Discover the "why" behind their disengagement.
- Complete a quick exercise where everyone writes an idea on a piece of paper, with the expectation they will share with the group.
- Give them a role in the meeting, like facilitator, notetaker, or timekeeper.

Conversation starters

- You are an important part of the success of our school/district and have so much to offer. What tips would you give the team to make this a productive meeting?
- What role would you like in our meeting today?
- You looked a little distracted during our PLC today. Is there something on your mind?
- Remember that one of our norms is to stay focused, limit side conversations, and have our laptops closed.

Derogatory

Looks like

- "I think this activity is stupid and useless."
- "I have to do this again? This is a worthless waste of my time."
- "I am not having 'that' kid in my classroom. You can't subject me to a year of drudgery."
- "I am going to call the superintendent and tell them you are not supporting me."
- "I think we should all meet after school and come up with a plan to sabotage this initiative."
- "I can't believe my teaching partner is such a suck-up to our department head, can you?"

Acknowledge/coach

- Create norms for meetings and hold people to them. One of our favorites is "praise publicly and criticize privately."
- Do not react in the moment. Find a private time to have a conversation after you have collected yourself and aren't feeling reactionary.
- Acknowledge their possible frustrations, but remind them of the purpose.
- Calmly and nonchalantly hand them your boss's number.

Conversation starters

- I see you are showing signs of frustration regarding the parent's lack of follow-through. How can we focus on their strengths to help the situation?
- What can we control at school to help your students grow?
- I value you as a team member, and would like to have a transparent conversation with you today. Tell me how you are feeling regarding . . .
- I am so sorry. (This can go a long way in calming someone down.)
- I wonder if you would be open to serving as a lab classroom for others?

Hard conversations are not for the faint of heart. They require an emotional intelligence they don't cover in principal school, but, man, are they worth it. Nothing feels quite as good as running into that parent in the hallway who smiles warmly at you, remembering last spring when she left a scathing message threatening to call the media on your lack of leadership. Hard conversations have the power to heal relationships. Hard conversations make communities stronger. Hard conversations ninety-nine out of a hundred times will make a situation better.

There are three basic principles to embrace as you go into this work:

1. Go in curious not furious
2. Presume positive intentions
3. Find commonalities

With these three practices firmly in place, you have the opportunity to lead through challenges and confront conflict with love, curiosity, and understanding.

> **Hard conversations make communities stronger.**

CURIOUS NOT FURIOUS

The late Dr. Joy Browne, a radio psychologist from New York, advised: "Go into conflict curious not furious." Isn't that great? Curiosity sparks wonder and leads to deeper understanding. If only everyone could go into difficult interactions with the goal of better understanding the other person's point of view. What a wonderful world it would be! "Curious not furious" is really about checking the emotion you are bringing to a situation. It means conducting a body scan of your breathing and blood pressure, and being more mindful of your thoughts. Doing so gives you feedback about whether you are ready to lead through a conversation or not. Very rarely in this work is there a discussion that cannot wait a few hours, or a day, or even a weekend, to give emotions time to cool off and allow you proceed with curiosity. Give yourself permission and space to wait if the timing isn't right. (Note: waiting is different than avoiding!)

When we are highly emotional, we have a tendency to be less log-ical. Consider how to *respond*, rather than react. Reflect on past con-versations to better understand how to set up future conversations for success. If you are not someone who can think quickly on your feet when confronted by anger, then it's probably not a best practice for you to meet with the parent who is yelling and shows up unannounced. Instead, greet them, tell them you would be happy to meet but now is not a good time. Schedule the meeting, plan out your questions, and go forward with a roadmap. Keep the goal in mind: it's not about solving the problem right this minute, it's about coming to a long-term solution.

"Curious not furious" is also about truly seeking to understand the perspective of others. It means asking good questions and not leading the conversation with your own agenda. Through that process, you often come away with a clear understanding of what the other per-son wants from the situation. In controlling your own reactions (the hardest part), it's important to have a bank of go-to questions to lean on when the conversation gets tough, such as: Can you tell me more about that? What is your perspective on why that happened? What solu-tion are you hoping for? By carefully crafting questions that help you understand the situation, you are able to better understand the other person's viewpoint and motivations in order to find solutions. "Curious not furious" also feels really good. You are not taking the emotions of the interaction personally, but listening attentively with a focus on solutions and understanding.

NONVERBAL CUES AND COMMUNICATION

Many of us are stewards of research, data, and best practices. However, to be a successful leader, you also need to be a student of nonverbal cues and communication styles. Some studies suggest that up to 93 percent of communication is nonverbal. It is not only your words, but your mannerisms, facial expression, and physical nuances that transfer messages. Our nonverbal communication is typically instinctive, so we may not be aware what we are conveying to other people. You may scratch your head, wondering why a conversation went awry. If you receive surprising reactions, examine your wordless signals, like your facial expressions or body position. You may be transmitting a very different message than what you are sharing verbally.

While we would love to expect and believe that people will tell us what's on their mind, extensive research shows that verbal communication is only the tip of the iceberg, and that we truly have to go deep with body language if we are to fully understand those around us. Perhaps you were a communication major during your undergrad years, and you took a nonverbal communication class. If so, you are extremely lucky. For those of us who didn't, learning these new skills can often feel like an uphill battle.

The good news is that reading nonverbal cues is a lot like learning how to drive a car: it just takes practice. At first it is extremely awkward, and you probably won't be very good at it; but over time, you become a master and, eventually, can do it proficiently without giving it your full attention. One book that Rachael has found incredibly helpful in understanding body language and what it means is *What Every BODY is Saying: An Ex-FBI Agent's Guide to Speed Reading People* by

Joe Navarro. While we aren't FBI agents, there is a lot to learned from how people respond to our questions and position their bodies when interacting with others.

PROVIDING SPACE TO RESPOND

Hand in hand with reading nonverbal cues is understanding and knowing when to allow space for a response. When you ask someone a question or are engaging in a difficult conversation, embrace the pause and allow for the other person to respond. Often, we are uncomfortable as we wait for a response, so we attempt to fill the space by expanding on the question we just asked, or by answering it ourselves. As much as we may think we are being helpful, we truly aren't. Instead, lead with grace and give the other person the time they need to speak from the heart and share what they truly mean. Another added benefit of offering space is that it gives you an opportunity to practice your newly developed nonverbal communication skills. However, a word of caution: Sometimes the space an individual needs won't be on your timeframe, and another meeting might be needed. This is ok. In fact, when you provide the time someone needs instead of forcing the conversation to continue, you are leading with grace, and the overall conversation will end in a much better place than if you had simply pushed through.

PRESUME POSITIVE INTENTIONS

Most people do not intend to be jerks, even when they may be acting like one. The parent who passionately demands her daughter be placed in a different classroom is not trying to dismantle your school community; at the core, she just wants what she believes is best for her daughter. (That doesn't mean she is right.) Presuming positive intentions in hard conversations is the second practice that will facilitate your success. Trust that the message, no matter how harsh, is coming from a good place. People are passionate because they care deeply. Caring deeply is a really good thing, especially when it is about children. If you can adjust your ears to hear beyond the words to the underlying message, you'll be able to discern someone's positive intent.

When you feel like you have identified this message, ask the person, warmly and empathetically, to confirm it: "It sounds like you really want your daughter to be happy at school, is that right?" "Are you feeling like your son isn't connecting with his teacher?" "I can tell that you care deeply about your child." This approach is also very important in staff conversations: "It sounds like you have tried a lot of things with this student, and it's still not working. Are you feeling frustrated by the lack of progress?" "I know you are working hard. This must be really challenging." Presuming positive intentions helps us remember that behind the conflict is a human being with human needs. Empathy and understanding help us stay in the light and navigate toward the positive.

Kate

Undoubtedly, one of my *favorite* things about my job is that I get to interact with amazing people on a daily basis. My staff and I talk about our favorite Netflix binges, exchange *People* magazines and Instant Pot recipes, celebrate milestones, and grieve losses. We hug often, say "I love you" all the time, and cry together on difficult days. When the synergy is pulsing and everyone is cohesive, we are a powerhouse. However, there are sixty-five of us and we *are* human. Sometimes we disagree, miscommunicate, resist change, and get snarky. That's when hard conversations need to occur.

Some people may think that the closer you are with someone, the harder it is to have difficult conversations. Recently, I had to have a tough conversation with a staff member whom I respect immensely as an educator, and whom I consider a friend. While I was receiving coaching from a trusted mentor about how to go about the exchange, she said, "This is going to be so awkward since you are friends." I said that, like any normal person, I was a little nervous, but I strongly believed that *because* of our personal and professional relationship, I owed this staff member an honest conversation. If I didn't care about this educator, I wouldn't spend so much time and effort preparing to have a productive dialogue. I believed in them enough to conscientiously hold them accountable to our high standards and to ask how I could participate in their growth as an educator. I respected them enough to be honest, direct, and engaged. I also loved them enough to show them that I believed in their potential, and to end our conversation with a hug.

FIND COMMONALITIES

There are always more commonalities than differences in human interactions. When leaning into hard conversations, listen for the things that can be agreed on, rather than those that cannot. The parent who wants to yell at you over a disciplinary situation at the core just wants their child to be safe at school. Guess what? You do, too. The staff member who is mad about the duty schedule wants their time to be valued and the master schedule to run smoothly. Guess what? You do, too. At the core of most problems lies a fundamental issue that everyone involved can agree on. When you are able to identify it, the conversation center on that agreement, rather than the argumentative details that get in the way.

In prioritizing commonalities, it is important to keep the conversation focused on the future, rather than the past. The future is something that can be agreed upon, while events in the past might be viewed from different perspectives. For example, when the parent who is angry enters your office to talk about the way a behavior referral was written at recess, chances are that, even after your investigation, there are going to be multiple perspectives from all involved. That said, you and the parent can agree that it is important for students to be safe on the playground and have trusted adults to check in with. The same is true for talking with staff members about performance after an observation. You might have persistent disagreements on the engagement of students during that particular lesson, but you can agree that engagement is important, and that you both want the teacher and the students to feel successful.

Focusing on commonalities keeps the conversation positive, hopeful, and grounded in genuine care and concern.

The most critical aspect of hard conversations is controlling your own emotions and actions. It takes practice and a lot of grace. Know that you are going to make mistakes and mess things up. Chances are there will be a topic that gets you emotional, your Achilles' heel, of sorts. Recognize it and mitigate it. Remember you don't always have to be by yourself in hard conversations. When appropriate, choose a side-kick from your building who will help you co-regulate your emotions. When you get stuck in a confrontation, you'll be able to toss the ball to them with a well-timed "What are your thoughts on this?" You and your wing-person can establish agreed upon signals to navigate the conversation. For example, if you have a tendency to get defensive, your partner could give you a little toe tap under the table. Sometimes it helps to have one person tend to the social emotional part of the conversation, while the other one takes the hard stance. The most important aspect of your dynamic duo is that you help each other have the most productive and respectful conversation possible.

When engaging in hard conversations, we recommend not making decisions on the fly. This is easily done when you don't allow yourself to be seen as the sole decision-maker. When decisions are made by a team, you can say, "That's an interesting solution, let me take it back to the team and get back to you," or "I wonder how that would work," or "Let me check in with X to see if there are any obstacles I'm not thinking of."

Many of us go into this role because we have good judgment, are decisive, and can see the big picture. These same qualities, however, can send things sideways when we engage in difficult conversations. This is a time when you need to take off your power hat in order to make room for the perspectives of others. In that space, you are setting the stage for relationships that will endure over time, which is far more important than any one decision.

SET THE STAGE

Consider ways that you can be intentional about setting the stage for collaboration and doing what is best for kids. In order to convey that you are open to listening, think about your environment: is your office warm and inviting, or cold and imposing? Think about the unintended messages that might be sent. The moment someone walks into the meeting space, they are gathering information about you and making assumptions and predictions. We all do it. Do you have objects such as books, quotes, posters, or décor in your office that communicate your philosophies? Aesthetics matter. They have the ability to soothe or intensify any given situation.

Be mindful when choosing the location for a meeting. Some need to be in your office, but others may be appropriate to have in the classroom, or even at a local coffee shop. Preserving people's dignity is critical. If a parent is ranting at the front office counter for all the gawkers to hear, remove them from the audience and invite them to a private conference area.

When settling in for your meeting, get out from behind your desk and sit next to the other person. Make sure your chairs are comfortable and that power is shared. In addition, whenever possible, include a third point of reference that makes the dialogue more tangible and less confrontational. This could be an agenda, data statements, evidence, or research. Making direct eye contact can be intimidating and uncomfortable. Placing data, a behavior referral, or observation notes between you and the other person can deflect intense energy.

TAP INTO EMOTIONAL INTELLIGENCE

Undoubtedly, hard conversations will bring emotions to the surface. Our defense mechanisms will be firing, and our instincts will be ready to take over. Although you may be upset, angry, sad, or defensive yourself, take a deep breath and tap into your emotional intelligence. Instead of taking the stubborn, inflexible, "show them who is boss" stance, choose kindness. Let's face it, it is really difficult to be mad at someone who is being nice to you.

Consider how genuine kindness may be used to melt anger. Pausing to give a person a sincere compliment may shift their mood. Think about sharing with a parent something you love about their child, or how you appreciate their involvement in site council. Asking about something important to them, like the outcome of a sports game or where they got their hair done, might lower their anxiety. Perhaps an inquiry about how their grandmother is feeling after her surgery or asking them to tell you about their favorite Hulu show just might put them in a different frame of mind and open up a more positive interaction. It is difficult to be mad at someone who just told you that their child gives the best hugs or is such a great helper or jumped twenty points on their reading assessment. Also, never underestimate offering a piece of chocolate, a bottle of water, or a cup of tea. It just may be the pause that will enable you to have a productive conversation.

STAYING GROUNDED AND KEEPING EXPECTATIONS REALISTIC

Gossip and rumors can grow and infiltrate school culture in negative ways. As the leader, you sometimes hear things indirectly, which is an awesome opportunity to lean into a hard conversation. Consider the power in saying, "Hey, do you have a couple of minutes? I heard something and want to gain additional insights from you?" Then going into the conversation with information-gathering prompts, like:

- How do you think my communication about that was received?
- Tell me your perspective on . . .
- Do you think I misinterpreted . . . ?
- What do you think will help us get beyond this?

When these conversations are neglected and ignored, they can fester and build walls between staff members. Something that starts small then becomes a huge obstacle that could have been avoided. When the goal is not about being right, but about building community, it's easier for everyone to agree on an outcome. In addition, if your staff knows you will follow up on pervasive gossip, they may be less likely to do it.

There will be times when you need to deliver tough information that cannot be negotiated. These conversations are the most difficult. Leading with care and concern is still central to navigating through them. Starting the conversation with the below sentence frames will help you navigate them:

- I need to have a hard conversation with you about . . .
- It's not the outcome you were hoping for, but these are the reasons why . . .
- I know you are passionate about this topic. I understand that you want this to happen and . . .
- In this circumstance that's not possible because . . .

Remember, there is no reason to gloat. There is no benefit in posturing. When someone responds with emotion, go in softer, not harder: "I see you are upset. Do you need a break?" Being a strong leader isn't about always making popular decisions, but when you make decisions that are consistent with your mission and communicate them with care and empathy, you will build relationships in ways that profoundly strengthen your community.

On rare occasions, no matter your best attempts, conversations go south—and sometimes badly. When you notice this happening, put a stop to it before it's too late. It is better to say, "Listen, I feel like we need to reschedule in order to have the whole team here," or "I want this conversation to be positive, and in order to do that, we need to both agree to speak to each other with respect. If that's not possible today, let's reschedule." Pushing pause on the conversation is much better than pushing through when emotions and conflicts are running hot. Notice in the language that we aren't suggesting you say, "You are being disrespectful. You cannot talk to us that way." Those types of accusations make things worse rather than better. Instead consider saying, "Listen, I can see you are upset. I need our staff to feel respected in this conversation, so I cannot continue the meeting if you use that language with her." It sets a firm boundary, but does so with respect.

LISTENING IS THE KEY

Listening is just as important as speaking in hard conversations. By seeking to understand multiple perspectives, you have the opportunity to learn more about the situation at hand, and gain deeper insights that will strengthen your relationship. It is so much easier said than done, especially when emotions run high and strong feelings are prevalent. When the parent who is animated across the table accuses a teacher of playing favorites in her discipline system and suggests that you are in the profession for the money alone, it is so hard to bite your tongue. The wisdom of Maya Angelou serves well in this moment: "People will forget what you said, people will forget what you did, but people will never forget how you made them feel." When you can make people feel heard and cared for in the midst of an awful situation, that is strength and leadership that will be remembered.

The key to deep listening is first to attune to your own emotional state. Sometimes it is better to delay the meeting to give time for those initial feelings to pass. While so much of what we do feels emergent, there are few things that cannot wait twenty-four hours for a more brain-friendly conversation when everyone is calm. In conversations, it is good to go in with a goal of listening 70 percent of the time, speaking 20 percent of the time, and asking questions 10 percent of the time. The questions you generate should be open ended: Will you tell me more about . . . ? How would you like to see this resolved? What else would you like me to know? When you listen well, you convey empathy and understanding. This does not mean that you agree with the other person. Saying things like "I can tell that you care deeply about . . . " and "I genuinely appreciate you sharing this information with me" can help build relationships in challenging situations.

———————————— *Kourtney* ————————————

Some of my best relationships in the building started a little rough and have been improved through hard conversations. At one point, I had a teacher who was visibly frustrated with me, but wasn't coming to talk to me about it. I had heard through the grapevine that this was because of the way I had handled a disciplinary situation where she felt like I hadn't backed her up. In the hallway, she would smile professionally at me, but the warmth was missing. I could have ignored it and moved on, but it bugged me.

One day after school, I said, "Hey, do you have five minutes? Can we chat?" She came into my office and we sat across from each other. I started with a soft opening: "I could be totally imagining this, but it feels like you are upset with me, and I just want to know if there is anything I did to hurt your feelings." She looked taken off guard and quickly said, "No, nothing." Knowing the grapevine gossip, I said, "Okay, the thing is that if there is something that's not right, know that I really want to make it better. I'd rather have a few minutes of awkward conversation that makes our team stronger than weeks of you feeling bad without me knowing."

The next day she came in and asked if she could talk with me. She unloaded A LOT about what I had been doing that bothered her, that was different from the previous principal, or that went against her personal philosophies. I kept asking questions, clarifying, thanking her for the information. When she came up for air, I led with gratitude. "Thank you for telling me the hard things. I really appreciate knowing this." I asked her if I could share some of my perspectives, and she agreed. We came out of that conversation with a better understanding of one another. We learned how to navigate our relationship and partner together for our kids.

She became one of my go-to people on staff. I could float ideas past her, and she would help me navigate the obstacles I couldn't see. What we learned from that pivotal conversation was that both of us were leading with heart, we both wanted what was best for kids, and we made a stronger team together than apart.

Hard conversations are critical for building a strong team. It starts by hiring the right person, who may not necessarily be your staff's first choice. Some of the most difficult discussions occur when a favorite substitute teacher/relative/best friend whom everyone on staff loves applies for a job, but you don't think they are the best fit for the open position. All of us have made wrong hiring decisions, and many times it is because we don't want to disappoint or anger someone. Trust us when we say that the students in your care deserve to have the very best person you can hire. The pain and awkwardness of having a difficult conversation with a disappointed staff member and/or applicant will be well worth the outcomes you will receive from hiring the right candidate.

When you convey a culture of listening, openness, and empathy, you can overcome any interpersonal obstacles. Don't forget: just like the oxygen mask on the airplane, these types of conversations require that, as leaders, we attend to ourselves first. You can't keep giving from an empty vessel, so self-care is vital, especially after a difficult conversation. Purposefully planning for the conversation and then taking care of yourself afterward will pay off in the long run.

Remember, go in curious not furious, presume positive intentions, and find common ground. With a focus on building relationships and fostering empathy, hard conversations can be transformative for your entire school community.

INVITATION TO IMPLEMENT

- Consider how to make your space more inviting and comfortable for hard conversations. Take a moment and look at your space through a new perspective. Invite a mentor, student, parent, or staff member to give you feedback.
- Facilitating hard conversations is a necessary skill to develop. Identify some go-to sentence frames for when you find yourself in these situations, like those below. Seek to understand by listening, and always be respectful.
  - Tell me more about . . .
  - What might it look like if . . . ?

- ○ Help me to understand . . .
- ○ How did it make you feel?

- Preparation is key. Consider practicing with a trusted confidant, keeping confidentially in mind.
- Craft a plan for how to prepare for these hard conversations so that they are collaborative in nature and end with positivity. Kindness and empathy go a long way.
  - ○ How can I best support you?
  - ○ Let me look into that and get back to you.
  - ○ What do you need as you move forward?
  - ○ I hear you are saying . . .
  - ○ I care about you.
  - ○ Thank you for being brave and vulnerable.
  - ○ I learned a lot from you today.
  - ○ Thank you for sharing.

CHAPTER NINE

DEVELOP YOUR NETWORK

"Widen the path of opportunities and continue to leave
a powerful and positive legacy in this world."

–Luis Fonsi

*D*id she just tell me that she was going to sue me and that I am not allowed to talk to her child as I investigate this incident? Is this even feasible or legal, given the situation at hand? As the seconds loudly tick on the clock, you realize you have to somehow respond to the parent. This is when you find yourself longing for the days when you worked with a strong, collaborative teacher team, or in a larger building where perhaps you'd have access to another administrator to glean advice. Oh, those were the glory days. Now, as the single administrator, it is up to you to make these decisions and to find ways to respond in the moment . . . gulp.

The work of leadership can be isolating in many ways. Even in larger districts, ideas and energy can grow stagnant. Serving as a principal can be a very lonely job and if you aren't connected to others around you doing the same work; the stress of the job will take a toll on you. It can feel like the weight of the world is on your shoulders as you work to solve problems in your school community. The reality is that there are literally over one hundred thousand principals in the United States engaging in work that is similar to yours. Connecting to the collective wisdom of others not only leverages success, but helps you feel like you are not alone.

Over the years, the three of us have found that being connected educators and having solid networks has truly made the difference when it comes to our daily life and overall job satisfaction. By developing your professional network, you are choosing to seek out others who may be like-minded or who think differently and bring new perspectives to the work. Whether they are folks you know personally and can text your out-of-the-box thoughts, or virtual connections through social media, these lifelines help to stretch you professionally in ways that might not happen within your district. There is something satisfying about being able to share your war wounds with another administrator at the end of a rough day and hear their insights. It is also a relief to hear their struggles so you know you are not alone. Your network becomes a touchstone for reality checks and a sounding board for decision-making. In short, these people can help you keep your sanity in crazy times, because we all know that being an administrator can sometimes be absolutely nuts.

─────────────────────── Rachael ───────────────────────

I moved across the state of Oregon for my first principalship. Not only was I entering into a new job that I had never done before, but I was in a community that was very different from what I was used to. I remember coming home from work that first month and wondering again and again what I had signed up for. Challenges that I had never faced before were now staring me right in the eye. Plans of assistance, big drug busts, and bomb threats were the norm in my new district, but were far from it where I had come from. Knowing that my old support system could only do so much from a distance, I knew I needed to reach out to others going through similar challenges.

The other two middle school principals in my district consistently reached out to me to ask how things were going. Even though I was a first year principal and felt lost the majority of the time, they would call me to ask my opinion on things. The first time they did this, I thought they were crazy. Here were two principals who had been doing this job for many years, wondering what I thought and how I would handle something.

All in all, we worked together for three years as a middle school principal team. During those years, the three of us became best friends and were critical in helping each other grow and flourish. While there were challenges and arguments along the way, we always worked through them and we never pulled away. We embraced the hard conversations, even though they were uncomfortable, and we pushed each other to be better.

As a middle school team, our teachers began to consistently collaborate with grade-level and content teachers at the other buildings. Together, they analyzed data and created scope and sequences with built-in common formative assessments. Our buildings followed our lead in working together, and the gains were huge. Our final year together as a principal team, all three of our schools were ranked as level-five middle schools. This was the highest ranking you could earn in Oregon at the time, and we were the only district in the state to have all our middle schools functioning at that level.

When asked years later how that had happened and what the secret was, we all simply refer back to our collaboration and partnership. We celebrated as a team. We brainstormed as a team. When someone was out of line, we called each other out as a team. We did it all. I know without a doubt that if I hadn't had this support network during my first few years as a principal, I would not be where I am today.

Think about your network. Regardless of the size of your district or building, it is important to develop your network of colleagues. As you think back on whom you connect with, let's explore ways to build your support network or professional learning network (PLN) at a local, state, and national level.

- Whom do you connect with at your district or local level?
- Are there leaders across the state who have inspired you?
- Are there national educators who intrigue you?
- Create a list of professionals whom you value.

YOUR LOCAL NETWORK

As you develop your network locally, concentrate on attending local workshops, conferences, meetings, or virtual networking events. When you walk into a meeting at a district or regional level, do you sit only with people you know, or do you branch out and sit with new folks each time? We know that it is much easier and much more comfortable to sit with those we know, but what is this predictable behavior truly doing to develop your network? If you are attending a training, meeting, or workshop with your team, are you making sure to connect with colleagues during breaks or lunch? Even as little as saying hello and making conversation while you are in line for lunch can spark a connection and potential relationship later down the road. Who knows, they might be working in a district or building that has similar challenges or initiatives as yours. This casual interaction could turn into a great person to bounce ideas off of, or to pick their brain for ways to prevent possible issues.

Connecting with others at a local level can also happen through less formal avenues, such as getting together to have coffee to pitch a project, visiting other buildings to glean ideas, meeting up for lunch or dinner to brainstorm solutions, or just calling to check in. The three of us have found this to be the best way to develop your immediate network with those around you. If you don't have a relationship like this with others in your district, it is easy to start by reaching out and saying hello to other principals in your district. These conversations begin to build a foundation of friendship, collaboration, and collegiality.

Let's also talk about ways to connect with your network locally when we are in a virtual setting. For starters, keep an eye on your email, as offerings come prolifically. Perhaps the local educational service district is hosting a series of lunch and learns on hot topics in education, or the local reading council is coordinating book studies throughout the summer for educators on Zoom. There are plenty of virtual opportunities; you just have to keep your eye out for them and be brave enough to participate. Consider how you can connect with other local educators during these events, even though they take place through a virtual platform. Once you sign up, know that this is just the first step. When the event starts, note who is in the virtual room with you or who is sharing fabulous ideas in the chat box. Don't hesitate to send people a private chat complimenting them on their idea and asking to exchange contact information. Some of these talented educators are geographically right next door to you and would be incredible folks to help keep the growing and learning pulsing. For example, say you are on a webinar about culturally responsive teaching practices, and you notice the administrator from a nearby district is sharing fabulous ideas about how to implement the work within the building. This is a great observation, as they could be a solid resource for you as you dive into this work with your staff. Make sure to jot the educator's name down and see if you can figure out where they work. Once the event is done, send them a follow-up email noting where you virtually met and that you would like to talk further with them about x, y, or z.

We also would encourage you to actually interact with others during these virtual opportunities, instead of multitasking or having your video turned off. Active engagement within the process will result in deeper connections, which makes it easier to build relationships in a virtual setting. Ask questions. Use the chat box. When someone asks for thoughts or ideas, don't hesitate to share your thinking. The more you speak up—or type up—the more engaged you will be, and this will help pull others in, as well. Finally, when the local online event is all done, we encourage you to take a moment to reflect on what you learned and how you can build your network through these events. Reach out virtually to those you connected with, including the presenters, as this helps create those connections.

———————————— *Kourtney* ————————————

Sometimes great things happen by chance. It had never really crossed my mind to get involved with a professional organization. As it was, I was in over my head and drowning in the work in my building. On a random chance, I was asked to present with a colleague to a group of new principals at a conference. There I met the leadership crew of our professional organization and was asked if I would consider filling an open position. My off the cuff "sure, I'll check it out" turned out to be a pivotal moment, both personally and professionally.

The next three years I spent on the board were incredible. Not only was I able to attend both local and national conferences to expand my own learning, but I engaged in great conversations with other professionals who have since become lifelong friends.

Learning from these women (two of whom coauthored this book with me) helped me so much as a leader. We talked about different ways to organize systems, how to have conversations, ways to navigate hardship—basically, all the topics we are tackling in this book were first mulled over in hotel lounges. There is something so special when you connect to other people whose purpose matches yours, and who are moving the mission forward in similar but notably different ways. I wish these types of relationships for all new administrators. I do believe there is something special in networking outside of your immediate colleagues that pushes you professionally in an important way. Be brave, take the leap!

YOUR STATE NETWORK

While it is hard to be out of your building, expanding your horizons at least a few times a year is a must. All three of us have found significant importance and value in being active within our state association. This means attending conferences and workshops that market to the entire state. These events have developed into extensive networking opportunities for us over the years. For example, during Rachael's first year as a principal, when she attended the state's law conference, she only knew the colleagues who were from her district. Ten years later, the majority of the faces at the conference are familiar. All of this just by being there when conferences and state events occur, and by making an effort to connect with other participants.

Once you are comfortable showing up and being present, you'll be amazed at the opportunities that come your way. You will become more familiar with those leading your state association, and this can lead to incredible opportunities. By participating and volunteering to present at statewide conferences, the three of us we were able to become involved at the board level for the Oregon Elementary School Principals Association. In turn, our connections and growth possibilities grew exponentially.

When pondering how to build your network at the state level, think about the following questions:

- What state conferences work with your schedule? Which ones align with what you are currently working on in your building?
- When you get to the conference, how are you going to reach out and create ten new connections?
- How are you going to follow up with those you connected with?

Beyond just looking to participate in face-to-face events, we also encourage you to utilize virtual events held at the state level. Whether it is a women's networking group for leaders across the state, or a secondary Zoom call once a week to talk about distance learning, best practices, or other topics, participating in statewide events virtually is a must. You can do them while in the comfort of your own home office and save a ton of driving time!

After our governor closed schools due to COVID-19 in the spring of 2020, Kate and Rachael developed a weekly virtual Let's Talk series. Once a week they invited principals and educational leaders from around their state to learn about, brainstorm on, and collaborate around relevant topics. They asked participants what they wanted to talk about and incorporated their suggestions into the weekly series. Topics included everything from navigating virtual learning, to engaging difficult-to-reach families, to virtual staff appreciation, to self-care. Sometimes they enlisted guest speakers, while other times they relied on their own knowledge. This series was a grassroots effort to create a network to support leaders. We connected with other leaders from every corner of our state, and even attracted a few out-of-state educators, as well. It was rewarding to meet other leaders who were in the same uncharted territory and problem-solve together.

While we encourage you to sign up for the events, the key to developing your network through these events is to *actually* attend. Come on . . . How many of us have signed up for these kinds of events with good intentions, only to find later that we had forgotten them or overbooked ourselves, or that our eyes were crossed from already having been on Zoom all day.

One tip for keeping apprised of networking and learning opportunities offered in your state is to pay attention to your state association's Twitter account, Facebook page, website, and email communications. When you see an event come through your social media account, instead of pushing it aside and thinking you will come back to it later, either save the date or sign up right then and there. Yes, pull out your calendar and block out the time and fill out the registration form immediately. If the meeting information is included in the event announcement, we encourage you to embed the details within the calendar event, so that when the time comes to connect with others, you don't have to go scrambling and digging into the depths of your email account to find the Zoom link or access code. As you look to develop your network, statewide events are vital in helping make it wider and more diverse.

YOUR NATIONAL NETWORK

Developing your network at the national level looks a little different than it does at the local and state level. While it is always incredible to attend national events, such as Learning Forward, National Association of Elementary School Principals (NAESP), Association of Supervision and Curriculum Development (ASCD), or National Association of Secondary School Principals (NASSP), we know it can be expensive, and often challenging to coordinate. Some administrators we know have incredible administrative contracts that allow and fund attending a national conference, which may be specifically identified in the contract. For those of us who don't, we have to be a little more creative to make it work.

Below are some creative ways educators can attend national conferences:

- Use your frequent flier miles for air travel.
- Attend national conferences that land during your noncontract time or at other times of the year when students are not in the building.
- Make the conference part of your vacation by extending days on either end of the event.
- Travel with local friends so you can save on hotel costs by sharing rooms.
- Plan ahead. Many national organizations put out information on when and where their conferences will be held at least twelve months in advance. Knowing this can help when it comes to travel arrangements and finding great deals, or just simply saving money so you can go.

If you aren't able to physically attend a national conference, don't sweat it. There are lots of ways to connect with folks and develop your network even from afar. The most successful way we have found to do this has been through Twitter. If you aren't on Twitter, you need to be (more on this in the next section).

Twitter is also where you can keep up-to-date on what national events will also be held virtually. Just like many local and state organizations are shifting their platforms to include an online option, so are many national-level groups. As we look ahead, we are excited about some of the opportunities provided by NAESP's interactive webinars, NASSP's Town Hall conversations and virtual conferences, as well as ASCD's virtual events. The opportunities to connect with folks nationally through professional development and Twitter are endless right now. Search, sign up, and watch your network grow!

Rachael

I wasn't on Twitter until my third year as a principal, when I was looking to move to a different district. We had just scheduled a site visit, and the superintendent from that district was coming down to visit my building, meet with staff, and talk to kids. I wanted to be prepared, so I googled everything I could find on the superintendent. A few simple web searches brought up her Twitter account, which was public and all education based. As I read through the tweets, I got a strong sense of who she was as a leader and the direction her district was going in. Coincidentally, when I got to the most recent tweet she had sent, it was about coming and seeing me at my building. Of course, she hadn't used my name or the name of my school, but I was 100 percent confident that the site visit she had referenced on the same day and in the same area as mine was one of the same.

This experience really made me reflect on my digital footprint. It also made me realize that I could connect with all these educational leaders and authors at the tap of a finger as I started an account and began following people from all over the nation. Many of my favorite educational authors and organizations had a strong Twitter presence. I am pretty sure I spent an entire afternoon going down the rabbit hole of educational Twitter.

I came across some phenomenal leaders such as Beth Houf, Shelley Burgess, Amber Teamann, Melinda Miller, and Jessica Johnson. Little did I know, I was seriously going to need their help in the next few months when I landed an elementary principal job, which was exciting as I had previously been a middle school principal. While I knew I could do the job, it had been at least six years since I had stepped foot into an elementary building. Since we had relocated to another part of

Oregon, I didn't know anyone at the elementary level in my district or surrounding areas, and I didn't know who to turn to for help.

So, I turned to Twitter. Every time I wondered about something, I searched Twitter. When I was curious what back-to-school nights looked like, I headed over to Beth's, Amber's, Jessica's, or Melinda's Twitter profile. I distinctly remember sitting in my office that August after just being told I needed to do an ice cream social for students and families, and not having a clue what this would look like. Thank goodness Melinda Miller had just posted something about a pool party and popsicles, so I was able to get an idea of what it all entailed, how to advertise it to the elementary families, and other things to think about. This happened time and time again over my first few years at the elementary level. Although I didn't officially meet Jessica, Melinda, Amber, or Beth until many years later, I relied on them during those early years as if they worked right down the hall. To this day, I am not sure the three of them know the level of support they provided to me just by sharing and being present on social media. I seriously owe my first few years at the elementary level to Twitter.

TWITTER

As we've already proclaimed in the previous section, Twitter is an amazing resource. When Rachael was looking for a bank of PBIS lessons that had Kagan structures infused, she turned to Twitter and found Becky Ince-Hutton, who shared her entire Google Drive. When a connected campus and connected educator presentation was needed, she again looked to Twitter and had more than five presentations shared with her within an hour. Talk about helping others out and not having to reinvent the wheel. Whether you are looking to connect or get ideas, Twitter is key. You have the ability to interact with so many incredible leaders, authors, and thought partners with unique and out-of-the-box ideas. Using this platform to increase your network and your repertoire of strategies is worth your time. If you are new to Twitter, educators Brad Currie, Billy Krakower, and Scott Rocco wrote a book called *140 Twitter*

Tips for Educators that is worth reading. We've listed some educators we recommend following in the resources section in the back of the book. Make sure to check it out!

As you become familiar with Twitter and look to utilize the platform to grow your network, we encourage you to engage with the process. Create and share content. Utilize hashtags such as #PrincipalEDleaders, #KidsDeserveIt, #PrincipalsInAction, #LeadLAP, and many others. This helps you connect the content to different groups of people that are sharing similar material. We also encourage you to interact with other educators by responding to tweets, instead of just retweeting them. Consider commenting on material in a positive, constructive way, and contacting others through direct messages.

Don't be scared to connect. While you might be hesitant to create strong networks all through social media, don't be intimidated by its power. There are many educational leaders and speakers who originally started their initial supports and friendships over social media, only to be enriched when they met in person years down the road. In our time in history, being physically distanced is no excuse not to be connected to other educational leaders, so flip open your device and start making meaningful connections.

BOOK STUDIES

Book studies are also a key way to virtually build your network at the national level. If you keep an eye open on social media, you will see a plethora of opportunities come your way to join virtual book studies as new books are released or authors host events. Sometimes the events are held in a closed Facebook group, others take place on Zoom, or perhaps on Voxer. Whatever the platform, know that these events create an incredible opportunity to build a network that includes these fabulous authors, but also to connect with amazing educators who are learning about the same things you are. Take advantage of them.

CONNECTING THE OLD-FASHIONED WAY

It is important to be savvy with making connections in the world of social media, but don't underestimate networking the old fashioned way, face-to-face. Each time you are with a group of people, think about how you can glean information, share ideas or resources, or make a new friend. Networking can happen with a parent you see every day, a principal from a neighboring district, or a speaker from halfway across the world. Just like the dozens of other skills that leaders need in their toolbox, networking is a skill worthy of practicing and perfecting. It is an art form that morphs with every situation. There are times when we feel confident and secure and don't hesitate to put ourselves out there. Other times, even the most extroverted people may feel shy and out of place. It is a compelling dance that can energize you at times, or make you feel small and insignificant. Below are some helpful hints that will get your dance card filled.

When you enter a situation where you want to make connections, first scan the room. Instead of sitting by people you know, or being an isolated wallflower, sidle up to someone you don't know. Most people in our profession are friendly even though they may wait for someone to take the lead. A quick introduction can break the ice. Remember, a smile, a warm handshake, and a compliment go a long way. People generally *love* to talk about themselves, so have a few open-ended questions at your fingertips to get the conversation going. Connect your questions to why you may be at the same conference or meeting. Ask them to tell you about their community or one thing that they find most exciting in their current work. Remember, someone who is fearless asks a lot of questions. Think about your eye contact, proximity to the person, and nonverbal actions. If you have your nose in your phone, people will generally take the cue that you really aren't interested in getting to know them. Be present and genuinely listen to what the other person has to offer. Be mindful of how much you are talking versus asking questions versus listening. Notice the nonverbals and take your cues.

If you value the conversation and want to continue getting to know a particular person or learn about something they are doing, offer your contact information and make sure you share *why* you'd like to keep in touch. It is always a good practice to carry your business card so that you can easily exchange information. We are notorious for getting back to our buildings and allowing the pressures of our "to-dos" swallow us up. By the time we finally get around to going through our cloth tote bag with the thick folder from the conference, we barely remember the person's name chicken scratched on the notepad, let alone the topics that were of interest. Therefore, make it a goal to reach out, in some capacity, within the week. We recommend even putting a reminder in your calendar for a week after you met that includes the person's name, email, and phone number. When you do reach out, recognize that they may have conference amnesia, too, so reintroduce yourself and mention something interesting you heard or shared. There is a chance that the person won't get back to you. Remember it takes two to tango, and you can only control your steps, so don't feel hurt if the synergy just isn't there. Just twirl your way to the next person.

Kate

I have had the good fortune to work with a vibrantly united administrative team throughout my decades as a principal. While the faces have changed, one thing has stayed true: we are a family that is committed to one another and to the elevation of *all* the students in our school district. Void of competition, with the exception of which staff member gets their SafeSchools trainings completed first (wink, wink), our admin team shares ideas, practices, schedules, and strategies. Our flow of trust and sharing has not only developed organically, but through advocating for systems of collaboration and deliberate implementation of structures that foster communication, feedback, and learning.

There are nine elementary principals in our cohort, and we genuinely love to learn from each other. We appreciate one another so much that we implemented collaboration meetings every Wednesday morning during the summer and asked to extend our bimonthly administration meetings during the year by an hour. You know we value our time together if we are actually *extending* a meeting! We keep a running list of topics we want to discuss and ask principals to bring artifacts, resources, and strategies to share. This is networking at its best! While not all principals can make every extended learning time due to vacations and other obligations, we find this uninterrupted time to unite and collaborate is our favorite part of the week.

We also have a group of district office leaders who foster networking and inspiration among their leaders. Our boss man, Andy Long, has the superpower of connection and is the glue holding our network together. He is in each of our buildings a minimum of twice a month and notices pockets of brilliance. He then interweaves the talents of individual principals and staff leaders into our network to facilitate learning. He will invite educators to participate in fishbowl activities, where the school staff will hold equity, attendance, behavior, or data team meetings, and the other leaders from outside the school will observe and soak up the knowledge by watching and asking questions. This results in a tremendous amount of authentic and shared learning.

Our superintendent establishes vertical teaming with our elementary, middle, and high schools, along with district administrators. We complete teacher observations together in each of our schools to calibrate our feedback. The conversations are insightful, and we gain wisdom from each other. Another example of deliberate networking takes place when our curriculum department sets up systems to identify and collect data on change ideas. Brooke O'Neil is our queen of research and collective efficacy. She sets up our entire elementary administrative team to work toward a common goal, like math discourse, and has the expectation that we individually collect data via walkthroughs at our buildings. We then meet once a month to share trends and strategies to propel practices. We are also paired up with another school each year and partner with them to complete observations as a cross-building team. Each time we meet we observe one or two teachers who have graciously volunteered to "dare greatly." We then match viewed strategies to research and share how to stretch our practice. It has been invigorating to network with various school leaders and teachers to elevate our practice collectively.

Whether you are creating and building your network at the local, state, or national level, in a virtual or face-to-face setting, we encourage you to keep the connections going. As we've mentioned, reach out by dropping a note, sending an email, or making a phone call, and don't forget to also connect using social media. Don't hesitate to follow others on Twitter, friend request a fellow leader you meet in person or interact with during an online event, or join Facebook groups that are geared to the work you are doing. There are so many opportunities to build your network. Make yourself available and open to expanding your professional relationships.

Finally, if you are in a culture that is not globally collaborative, create your own system for networking. Invite colleagues to meet, set up a shared Google doc for ideas around a particular topic, and invite a fellow leader to go to a conference and road trip together. The key is to open the dialogue and break down the walls of competition. Nothing is as powerful as creating a welcoming culture of sharing, and it all starts with showing your own commitment to networking with others.

INVITATION TO IMPLEMENT

Take a moment to brainstorm your steps for developing your network:

- What is your first step?
  - What platform are you using to connect with people: in person, social media, online conferences or meetings, etc.?
- What is the timeline for taking your first step?
  - What are your short-term and long-term goals to keep connections relevant and ongoing?
- How are you going to foster the connections you make?
  - What are your plans to reach out and keep the conversation going?

- How are you going to follow up?
  - Schedule it and follow up.

Use an equity lens to review your network and consider ways to expand your perspectives to connect with others:

- Is there a diverse group of people who are extending your thinking and learning?
- Research people outside of your school district, your state, your region.

CHAPTER TEN

COMMIT TO YOUR LEARNING

"Don't be intimidated by what you don't know. That
can be your greatest strength and ensure that you
do things differently from everyone else."

–Sarah Blakely

It's 8:00 p.m., and you still haven't left your office yet. You've put
in your fortieth hour this week, and it is only Wednesday. As you
think about how you really need to get home to see your family, you
keep coming back to how many things you still need to get done, and
how tomorrow would go so much smoother if you could just get one
more thing accomplished. As you finally close your laptop and shuffle
out of the office, you find yourself dragging as you walk to the car. If you
make it home in one piece, it will be a miracle. You think to yourself, I
really should read Zaretta Hammond's *Culturally Responsive Teaching
and the Brain* when I get home, but I am just too tired. I guess it can
wait until July.

As you walk through the door at night, professional and personal
learning is probably the furthest thing from your mind. We get it. Being

a principal swallows up a lot of your time and energy. When you finally get a chance to rest, you truly want to turn it off and just watch Netflix, read *People* magazine, and throw a Frisbee to your dog. While this is often our go-to reaction, as well, having a solid commitment to learning is vital to becoming a successful and relevant leader.

ALWAYS KEEP LEARNING

We believe one of the things that makes great leaders rise is that they are always learning and growing. They have a defined and visible commitment to professional learning. Depending upon what research you examine, many sources say that people should be tackling an hour of professional or personal development a day, and average between five and seven hours a week. Michael Simmons, founder of Empact, an entrepreneurship firm, coined this term as the "five-hour rule," as he found that no matter how busy one might be, those who are successful spent at least one hour a day learning or practicing a new skill.

> We believe one of the things that makes great leaders rise is that they are always learning and growing.

When you think about incorporating an hour of learning into each day, it might feel a little overwhelming to say the least. We get that—especially when you are up to your eyeballs in a shift to distance learning from a traditional face-to-face model, or when you are just starting out in a new position. Let's start small and take just one step forward as we figure out how much time you are currently spending on learning. Consider your weekly schedule. How much time are you committing to your own intellectual growth? Look at your schedule and examine your daily tasks. How much information are you consuming by reading blogs, articles, or books to improve your practice? Ten minutes, twenty minutes? Jot it down. As you go through your week, how many minutes do you spend listening to podcasts or watching webinar events? Jot that down. As things come to mind, record them below with the estimated time you are currently spending. Remember that learning can look many different ways, so make sure to think outside of just reading books. Take a moment to reflect in the activity below.

Reflect on how you currently learn:

1.	Time Involved:
2.	Time Involved:
3.	Time Involved:
4.	Time Involved:

As you think about your current state of learning and how much time you are dedicating to your professional growth, think about how it fits into your daily, weekly, or monthly schedule. We encourage you to find ways to go deep. Can you incorporate learning into your morning or evening routine? How can you find time each day to grow your practice? Ideas for learning you can fit into any open time slot include: weekly newsletters, updates from your favorite bloggers or writers, (like the Marshall Memo or ASCD's SmartBrief), keeping a book with you at all times, installing the Kindle app on your phone with your current e-book downloaded, and having preloaded podcasts on your phone so you aren't dependent on having internet coverage. We also have a list of some great recommended resources you might find valuable as you continue your learning, which are located in the back of the book.

We preach the importance of reading to our students and staff, and it is important we heed our own advice with books, articles, and blogs. We truly can't express the importance of reading. While you might not have the time to devour a book within a week, two weeks, or even a month, the important part is that you are reading to grow and improve your practice. You might start with reading just ten minutes a day, and as you gain momentum, bump it up to twenty. As time goes on, you would be surprised with how quickly you finish a book.

While purchasing lots of books on your own can get expensive, you might consider allocating some building budget money or professional development dollars toward creating a professional development lending library for you, your staff, your families, and other leaders within your building or district. Another way to go about adding variety to your bookshelf could be by organizing a book swap at your next administration meeting. Still other ways to access books without killing your bank account or budget is by using your local library, going to a used bookstore, or signing up for the Kindle Unlimited program. Even if you don't have a Kindle device, you can download the app on your phone, tablet, or computer to access a wide variety of e-books, including topics on educational trends, leadership, personal enhancement, and self-care.

While reading is a fabulous start, it's also important to keep in mind *how* you are reading. Are you reading the pages with intention and with an eye to understand, or are you reading but only half present as you think about all the other things you need to be doing? While we have all "been there, done that" when it comes to distracted reading, it might be helpful to find a quiet place free of things that can pull you away from the text. These may include your phone, your Hulu channel, or busy home activities. As you read, reflect and ponder the content on the page, and don't hesitate to reach out to the authors of the blog, article, or book. Authors typically welcome constructive feedback, additional inquiries, and inquisitive questions. Most authors are very responsive to their readers. This includes the three of us!

I love the first two weeks of August. I return to work after a wonderful month with my family, well rested, vitamin D levels high, and ready to dream about the possibilities. The first weeks of August are a bit like long-distance dating: you only think about the positive stuff without the distractions of reality to cloud your view.

If you are anything like me, keeping instructional leadership and being the "lead learner" front and center is something that I'm 100 percent behind in August before school begins, and 25 percent action on in September, when the rubber hits the road. I decided that in order to make learning actionable, I needed to create a system to sustain it.

Every day part of my routine is to email out the staff absences. One email, every day. I decided to take advantage of that daily point of contact to add a monthly instructional focus and weekly reflection. In August, when I was bright and shiny, I identified a list of instructional focuses that aligned with high-leverage strategies according to John Hattie's effect sizes on student achievement. Here are some of my favorites from my list:

- Collective teacher efficacy
- Relationships
- High expectations
- Lesson design
- Feedback
- Personalized learning goals
- Metacognition
- Personalization of learning
- Teacher clarity
- Student talk versus teacher talk
- Collaborative learning

- Celebrating success

For my monthly instructional focus, I would research articles or videos on the selected topic and link to them in my morning email. Then, each week, I would include quotes from research and reflection questions to help spark deeper thinking on the topic. When I walked through the building, I would look for the instructional focus in action and give shout-outs to staff. Here's an example:

Monthly Focus

Learning is a personal process. This month let's focus on the personalization of learning. This means personal connections, personal interests, personal feedback, personal goals. How can we increase our impact on student learning by deeply knowing and communicating with our students? How might this increase engagement and student outcomes? If you want to learn more, here is an article that might interest you, or this video on the topic.

Reflection

The personalization of learning includes blending student interests into the classroom. How can you solicit information from your students to better understand what they want to learn about and what they are passionate about? Consider ways to get the right books into their hands, to use these topics in the articles you choose for close reading, and to develop math problems that incorporate their interests. All of these strategies help boost engagement and make learning meaningful. It first starts by knowing your students on a personal level.

Quotes of the Week

"If teachers don't know the hopes, dreams and interests of their students, it's pretty hard for them to construct what's going on in the classroom, so that students see it in their self-interest to be self-engaged." —Larry Ferlazzo

"In the end, your legacy won't be about your success; it will be about your significance and the impact you made on every student, every day, and whether you were willing to do whatever it took to inspire them to be more than they ever thought possible." —Jimmy Casas

"Culturally responsive teaching isn't a set of engagement strategies you use on students. Instead, think of it as a mindset, a way of looking at the world. Too often, we focus on only doing something to culturally and linguistically diverse students without changing ourselves, especially when our students are dependent learners who are not able to access their full academic potential on their own." —Zaretta Hammond

Greatness in Our Midst

(This is where I would give a shout-out to staff members who are rocking it in this area!)

The best thing about this strategy is that it kept me focused on instructional leadership in my building. Each month I started by researching the topic and finding recent articles or videos that helped to illustrate it. It centered my own focus. There were times when I deviated from my August plan based on the needs of the building at the time, but the August hopes and dreams were able to come with me through the challenges of the seasons.

Block the time out

Outside of fitting professional development into some of your open timeslots, we invite you to block some time out each week or throughout the month for learning. If you know of a special event happening that you want to attend, put it in your calendar and plan ahead. Whether that be a book club of educational leaders that meets on Zoom every Monday evening, or a Twitter chat that happens every other week, put it in your calendar and plan on attending. Some principals we know actually block time out to learn during the school day. Sometimes they take their learning with them for when they visit classrooms, and other times they do it right after the day starts or lunch ends. Lifelong learning is a critical practice to model for students and staff. Through trial and error, we have found that the more we plan for professional enhancement and build our schedules to support our development, the more likely it is to happen. After all, our schedule reflects what is most important to us.

Recorded events

Even if you don't have the time or ability to participate in professional development in real time, whether from family obligations, conflicting meetings, or even being in a different time zone, don't let it stop you. Check to see if the event will be recorded so you can access it later. Get Your Lead On, NAESP's series of events and webinars, and many other great professional development opportunities record their events. You can log on later to access the learning, when it fits your schedule. Perhaps you can listen to the webinar or the keynote speakers as you are driving into work, doing yard work, taking a walk around the neighborhood, or relaxing once your kids go to bed. While it isn't the same as experiencing it live, it is better than opting out of the event and the learning entirely.

Follow the hashtag

You might also find some value and benefit from following the hashtag of the event. There have been times we haven't been able to attend professional development events, either virtually or face-to-face. Instead, we Twitter-stalk the hashtag of the event and are able to feel as if we were there when thought leaders shared their powerful points and material in real time. This is also something you can go back and do after the event, as well, whether it's with a speaker, Twitter chat, or an in-person or virtual conference. Remember, don't let time be a road block. There are lots of ways around it!

Learning with friends

There is power in numbers when it comes to learning. Sure, it is fun to learn, but it is even better when we can do so with friends and colleagues. As you think about your plan for continued professional development, consider how you can include others. If you are participating in a book study you know a friend would enjoy, invite them. If you were just talking to a fellow leader about an online symposium you saw, share it with them. The more we can attend in groups and numbers, the more powerful the learning will be. Learning in isolation can be helpful, as it allows you to dive deep into areas that interest you; but having others with you on the journey will have a lasting impact to your learning and add depth and richness to your experiences through exposure to fresh perspectives and ideas.

You might also consider creating your own learning opportunities within your networks. If you are diving deep on a topic, invite others to grow with you. Are there colleagues you could meet up with to share in the learning experience? Could the book you are reading on your own be used for an administrative book study during the summer? Perhaps you could invite your staff or parent group to join you in summer reading. Just because it isn't currently being offered by someone else, doesn't mean it can't or shouldn't exist. Instead create it and share the opportunity with your staff, families, communities, and networks. Whether you choose to do this through email, social media, or other modes of communication, you will be surprised by the level of interest. Even if folks don't join, at least you provided them an opportunity to collaborate and grow.

How to focus

How do you determine you learning priorities? That is the million-dollar question. We have found success by thinking about our learning with two different lenses. One, what do I need to learn about right now? Two, what do I need to learn about so I will be one step ahead of where I want to take my staff? Thinking about learning with these two different points of view will help you sift and sort through the millions of available books and resources so you can best put them to use. Without implementing a system, we are like leaves in the wind, blowing from one direction to another as a new book is released, the latest and greatest instructional strategy comes out, or a tweet goes viral.

When you consider what you need to learn right now, reflect on what knowledge will bring you up to speed with current ideas, or what might be holding you back. For some, this might be a technical knowledge skill. Perhaps you just took a job in a district that is heavily steeped with response to intervention (RTI), and you have little experience in this area. Or maybe you have incredible technical knowledge, but you need to work on your people skills and on understanding what makes people tick. Whatever it is, some self-reflection will benefit you as you look to narrow down your area of learning.

Rachael

"Rachael, you are one of the smartest people I know," my supervisor told me recently, when we were in the middle of caucusing as an administrative team for classified contract negotiations. "There is no question about that. Instead of always working on developing your technical knowledge, you might think about working on how to interact with others. You need to start learning and reading books about people. Be a student of the people around you. Study what makes them tick and what motivates them. That, Rachael, will get you further than knowing the effect size of an instructional strategy, and what a solid response to intervention system looks like."

Wow. This statement took me aback, as it was out of the blue. I am pretty sure I just froze with my mouth open and stared at him for a few minutes. There were things that had happened in the bargaining room with various dynamics and body language that I hadn't even picked up on. I completely missed them. I closed my mouth and began to nod. My supervisor is a master at working with others and getting them to do what is needed. He is a pro at communicating and understanding how to motivate others. And, of course, he was right.

As I reflected on the books I was reading and the content I was up to my eyeballs in, none of it was about emotional intelligence, communicating, or how to read people. Realizing this was indeed an area I needed to develop, I ordered some books and downloaded audio books on Audible that I could listen to while driving or out on a walk. As I jumped into these new books, it became even more apparent why my supervisor had made the suggestion, and I started to see how it could help me move forward with my practice.

Once you have a plan for working on your immediate situation, your next step is to figure out where you are going. We already talked about this in our chapter on clarifying your purpose but the next step in this growth process is to gain the knowledge you need to make gains as a staff or individual. Take a moment and reflect: Where do you see your community in five years? Where do you see it in three years? How about next year? We encourage you to also think about where you see yourself in the future. Do you imagine yourself moving on to the district office in a director role? Perhaps you want to be the human resources director or be in charge of curriculum. Whatever it is, you need to know where you are going so that you can start learning and developing the skills you need for the future. If you don't plan ahead, you will be behind the eight ball when it comes to changing jobs or approaching a challenge you knew you would ultimately be facing. Take a moment and write down where you see yourself and your community in the future so you can create a vision and path for learning as you move forward.

Five years:
Three years:
Next year:

Kate

Several years ago, my staff took on a new professional learning model called "lesson study." This format includes microplanning a lesson with a group of colleagues, with one of you then teaching the lesson to a group of students. The other colleagues observe and take notes on how the lesson elicits engagement and a hierarchy of responses. Afterward, the team shares notes and tweaks the lesson. The same teacher would then reteach the modified lesson to a second group of students, and the team would decide how the changes improved the level of engagement and response.

As the leader of the building, I was asking my staff to try something new to improve their craft. I therefore chose to be part of every step of the process. This included volunteering to be the teacher. Over two years, I repeated this process in every grade level.

Yes, it was time-consuming, and the emails piled up, but it was also one of the most profound learning experiences of my career. Not only did it add to my strategy toolbox, it provided insights as to the time it took for our teachers to plan, organize, and implement lessons. It gave me a deeper understanding of how our teams collaborated with each other and how to capitalize on their strengths. It leveled the playing field and increased the trust between the teachers and me, because part of the process was analyzing and giving feedback on each lesson taught. It made me feel vulnerable. I'll admit that, at one point, I even cried; thankfully, my team was incredibly supportive.

Getting into that trench with your teachers is a risk, but a risk worth taking. It is an opportunity to show your commitment to your own learning, no matter how messy it may become. Taking risks with your staff will bring you closer together, build trust, and ultimately grow your practice together.

Finally, we invite you to keep in mind that learning also comes through your relationships and connections with the people who surround you on a regular basis. Seek out the professionals in your immediate sphere, as well as those who hold higher positions, for growth opportunities. Inquire about the bigger picture and the "why" behind a particular decision. Go into the conversation with a sense of curiosity and explain that you would like to understand the decision for your own growth. Comprehending the broader spectrum helps us develop our knowledge base and skill set in our current positions, which will undoubtedly help us in the future. Are there people you could consistently connect with to gain knowledge? Perhaps this person is your director at the district office, your superintendent, the technology director, or a principal at a different level. Remember, knowledge could be waiting across the hall. You just need to spend the time and effort to tap it.

INVITATION TO IMPLEMENT

Commit to your learning! Take a moment to craft your plan:

- How are you going to fit learning into your daily, weekly, monthly, and yearly schedule?
- How are you going to seek out the information you want/need?
- What are you going to learn about that will meet your immediate needs?
- What are you going to learn about that will support your building's focus areas for the upcoming year?

— PART FOUR—

CARE

CHAPTER ELEVEN

FIND YOUR BALANCE

"We need to do a better job of putting ourselves
higher on our own 'to-do' list"

–Michelle Obama

*B*alance. Let's face it: some of us do a stellar job at balancing work, family, friends, health, and the million other things occurring in our daily lives at any given moment, and some of us applaud ourselves for actually taking the time to pop five Wheat Thins in our mouth and chase them with a flat Diet Pepsi for lunch. When some of us started our career there was no talk of balance. During these dark ages, you prided yourself on never taking a sick day. You were the first to arrive at work and the last to leave. By golly, you didn't even know where the staff room was located because you tutored students during your twenty-eight-minute lunch every day. Yes, you may claim your place in *Guinness World Records* for having the largest and strongest bladder, but at the end of the day, are you your best you, and is this breakneck pace sustainable?

"If you aren't careful, this job will eat you alive." The three of us have talked about this phrase frequently over the years as we have worked to find our stride and thrive in the workplace, while also keeping the rest of our lives in balance. We need to find that balance and we need to take care of ourselves so we can help take care of others. After all, if you aren't taking care of yourself, you *can't* take care of others. And we all have so many people worthy of our strong support.

Over the years we have come to realize that chronic stress goes hand in hand with being a principal—that is, if you allow it. Once stress gets a grip on you, it starts to creep its way into your sleep schedule, your eating habits, the time you spend with friends and family, and most importantly, your health. Stress is sneaky like that. You start to feel stressed during the day, and you reach for a Red Bull and the old Halloween candy at the bottom of your desk drawer. You work fourteen to sixteen hours a day, and you don't have time to work out because that would cut into your time with your kids or spouse. Or perhaps you've been needing to go to the doctor because you aren't feeling well, but you just can't seem to find the time to get there or even make the appointment. This is the life of many educational leaders, but it doesn't have to be. There is hope, and you'd be surprised how much better you could feel with just a few small changes.

Kourtney

People have described me as calm. I am at my best in the midst of chaos: able to triage, make decisions, and prioritize in the middle of a crisis. I come home to a busy family, and I have a serious fear of missing out, so I make sure to arrange my schedule so that I rarely do. I am like so many of us in these roles: I do all the things all the time.

I started to notice little signs that things weren't as picture-perfect as my Facebook profile might suggest. My hair had started to fall out in concerning webs, my muscles ached, I couldn't sleep, relaxation felt foreign, and I sensed fatigue deep in my bones. I finally went to my doctor when I started having heart palpitations, a quickening of my heart rate that would occur randomly as I sat at my desk. She put me through tests as I searched through the darkness of possible medical diagnoses on the web and thought about *Beaches*, my favorite movie growing up. (Why do we do this to ourselves?!)

After a month of tests, my doctor was happy to report that there was nothing physically wrong with my heart. Then she tilted her head, smiled knowingly, and said, "Tell me about your stress level." She referred me to a naturopath who specialized in this area. I took a test measuring my stress hormone levels, which as you might imagine, were off the charts. I was calm and cool on the outside, with a cortisol hurricane wreaking havoc on the inside.

The solution was to shift my priorities. In caring for others, I needed to also care for myself. It was not new information, but funny how a racing heart and throbbing neck vein can all of a sudden make it compelling to follow. I scheduled yoga, returned to church, put limits on my work/home balance, and committed to practicing some self-care. Like anything worthwhile, it's a journey, not a race; I had to recognize that stressful living is my preferred way of being. I seek it out, and it feels good to be needed. Like too much of anything, it can go from good to bad really quick.

For me, it's not about balance anymore. "Balance" makes me think of delicately preventing a precarious stack of things from falling, and that feels too tense to be sustainable. Instead, I think of the calming predictability of Newton's swinging cradle. It's not so much about balance as it is as being that middle ball: completely centered and present wherever you are.

This idea of maintaining your health connects back to Maslow's hierarchy of needs. As a leader, you must make sure that even the needs at the most basic levels are being met. We need to make sure we are eating healthy and consistently throughout the day, that we are drinking enough water (not just living on coffee and other forms of caffeine), and that we are rested. While it might feel silly to be talking about Maslow's foundational level of need since we are educators and we already know all this; but do we know it well enough to reflect on how it applies to us personally? When you check in with your fellow leaders at your monthly admin meeting, how many of them respond that they are tired, stressed, or didn't get lunch? Are they combatting their circumstance by guzzling a quad-shot black Americano, or by getting eight hours of sleep? This is a familiar interaction for us. Here's the thing: You can be rested. You can eat healthy throughout the day and workout each day if you want. You don't have to pick your job over your health. You can have both!

> You don't have to pick your job over your health. You can have both!

Kate

I will be the first to admit that I don't balance well, and I am a work-aholic. I grew up in a household where work ethic was highly regarded. As the daughter of an ex-marine, the harder you worked, the more praise you received. Sick days were for wimps and anything less than a ten-hour day was laughable. If something was worth doing, it was worth doing it well. You held yourself to the highest standards, and when you fell, you got up quickly, brushed yourself off and got right back in the game. There was no time to pause. There was no time to be vulnerable or show weakness. We just worked; and when things weren't going well, we worked harder. Like many of us, these child-hood expectations have woven into the threads of my adult life and career. Like any strength, my dedication and work ethic have lead me to many successes—but at what cost?

My cost has metastasized in my stooped shoulders and the lum-bering weight of extra pounds. The cost is seen in the crevice between my eyebrows and the coarse silver hairs that spring from my scalp. The costs are not only physical, but also relational. There have been many nights when I was a shell of a person with my family: physically present, but unavailable. Instead of taking walks to enjoy breathing the crisp air, I felt compelled to flip open the laptop and answer just a few more emails in the glow of a screen. While my work ethic told me to keep trudging, it was harder and harder to stay healthy.

As with most addictions, I struggle with balance every day. Some seasons I eat healthier, walk a little more, and slumber a bit more peacefully. Other times, the demons drag me down until I am choking on getting one more thing accomplished.

Last spring was one of those times that I was drowning in my vat of work, when our district offered a series of Mindful Leaders networking events for principal-leaders. The sessions were being led by Lana Penley, a practicing principal in a neighboring school district, who had recently started Mindflow, a company that focuses training others in mindful practices. Admittedly, I sat through that first session with Lana thinking all the belly-breathing and chime time stuff was ridiculous. In the time it took her to lead us through the exercises to clear our minds, I had my whole staff agenda planned out in my head and had made my grocery list, to boot. Needless to say, I wasn't sold on all this mindful mumbo jumbo after that first session—but I did come back the next month, and the month after that. By the end of our time together, she had taught us so much about self-care, balance, gratitude, and mindfulness. I was so hooked on these practices that I couldn't wait to bring her in to engage my staff in the same process, so they, too, could find more equilibrium in their world.

One of the activities Lana used with my leadership group was to read the poem "Fire" by Judy Brown. I think it speaks profoundly to the topic of balance. As you read it, highlight the words and lines that resonate with you and write a few notes in the margins about how it connects to your world.

FIRE

What makes a fire burn
is space between the logs,
a breathing space.
Too much of a good thing,
too many logs
packed in too tight

can douse the flames
almost as surely
as a pail of water would.
So building fires
requires attention
to the spaces in between,
as much as to the wood.
When we are able to build
open spaces
in the same way
we have learned
to pile on the logs,
then we can come to see how
it is fuel, and absence of the fuel
together, that make fire possible.
We only need to lay a log
lightly from time to time.
A fire
grows
simply because the space is there,
with openings
in which the flame
that knows just how it wants to burn
can find its way.
— Judy Brown

Why is maintaining your health is important? For starters, you are not dispensable. The students, the staff, and the families need you. Whether or not you believe this to be true, you are in your position, experiencing your current challenges for a reason. You might not know the greater "why" at the present moment but it is there. If you aren't taking care of yourself early on in your career, the impacts can be much larger and more severe later down the road. For example, every winter, many of us are faced with the decision to stay home or go to work when we are sick. For a lot of us, the impulse is to always go to work. We drag ourselves into the building, coughing, sneezing, and running a low-grade fever as we limp along toward the weekend with the hope that we can rest and get more sleep once students leave the building Friday afternoon. While we might be able to get away with doing this in the short term, it isn't a good habit to create, as it can and will kick you in the butt when you don't get better, and you end up missing a full week instead of just the two days you would have missed if you had stayed home in the first place.

Maintaining your health on a daily basis is just as important when you look at the end game. Many educational leaders throughout the nation find themselves with high levels of stress and not-so-hot habits for health. This creates a situation where we may have high blood pressure, be overweight, and/or be prime candidates for heart disease and other health issues. As leaders, we need to take the time to go in and get our annual checkups. We need to make the effort to schedule doctor's appointments during the day, even when that means we have to take a day off from work, and not ignore the follow-up when we find that lump, bump, or abnormal occurrence going on within our bodies. The more we embrace taking care of ourselves, the longer we kick the can down the road of leading a long, happy, healthy life in which we are positively impacting the children in our community.

While you might not be able to avoid every germ, especially as you high-five all those wonderful kids as they enter the building each morning, there are ways you can help ensure that you are staying healthy and at the top of your game. As a rule of thumb, you need six to eight hours of sleep each night. If you have trouble getting to sleep, try turning off technology and anything with a blue light at least one hour prior to going to bed. Charging your phone in another room is also a smart move, so it won't be there to pick up as you try to nod off.

ROCKING YOUR MORNING ROUTINE

When you wake up, do you automatically pick up your phone to check who has texted to say they are out sick and can't find a sub, what's been posted on Facebook about your school or community overnight, or how many fires you already have burning in your inbox, right out of the gate? While this habit might appear as if it's part of prepping for our day, it in fact steals some of your best and most productive hours. In his book *The Miracle Morning*, success coach Hal Elrod recommends that you start your day with affirmations, visualization, exercise, reading, journaling, and some silence. If you master your morning and start off on the right foot, he says, the level of success you will see as the day progresses will be higher than if you roll out of bed, check your phone, and then get ready to head into work.

MOVING YOUR BODY

We know, we know . . . There is never enough time in the day. How do you find the time to have a rocking morning routine when you are already short on time? As motivational speaker Rachel Hollis would put it: get up one hour early. She recommends that you move your body each day for at least thirty minutes, and then spend the other thirty minutes working on you, which is right where your Miracle Morning routine fits right in. If you aren't able to work out in the morning (which, honestly, not everyone is a fan of, but Rachael totally is), you might try to find some time in the afternoon to help you decompress from the day with an activity you enjoy. For example, Kourtney doesn't like to run, but does like to do yoga, so she does it in the evenings. Kate, on the other hand, likes to get her ten thousand steps in by visiting classrooms throughout the day. Whatever it is you like to do to move your body, do it! You do you—just make sure you are getting in some exercise and taking time for yourself.

So, take a moment and make a plan. How can you get your body moving, and when can you fit it in?

Possible exercise:

1.	
2.	
3.	
4.	

Rachael

"Dude, you need to start working out again!" This came from my husband right after I went off about how my day had gone, and I'm sure there wasn't anything positive included in my forty-five-minute tirade. I was taken aback by this direct statement, which had nothing to do with what I had just been talking about and made me wonder about the motivation behind it. Was I gaining weight? Did I look like I needed to work out? There were so many ways I could spin it, and most of it didn't come from a positive place. After some pointed questions from me, my husband clarified that I am a much nicer person and deal with work stress more easily when I work out consistently. Seriously?! That was a shock and a little hard to hear. After trying to debate with him about how I didn't have time, since I needed to be at work by 6:45 a.m., and meetings often went late into the evening, he told me that I was just going to have to deal with it and start getting up early to run. Fine. I honestly figured that I would give it a try for a few weeks so I could get him off my back, and soon I would be able to show him that it's just the nature of the job; it wasn't me, and it had nothing to do with working out. Welcome back to sleeping in . . . here I come.

Little did I know that after a few weeks of rolling out of bed and running consistently, I would feel so much better and would actually like work again. It's interesting, because people started to notice. They noticed that I had more energy at work. They noticed that I had more patience. They noticed that I was able to take challenges in stride instead of losing my marbles. After the third person asked me what I was doing differently, it dawned on me that it was the running and my husband had been right. Darn it!

As the months progressed and my running continued, I started to find that I was so much more emotionally stable, and was a much better principal. I even found myself adding in a second workout when I got home, either doing a spin class, exercise video, walking, or lifting weights. This was gold. The morning workouts set me up for success in my day, and the evening workouts help me take the edge off, so I can leave it all behind when I engage with my family and friends. This journey of health and fitness has been a huge game changer for me. To date, I have been running 100 plus miles each month since October 2018, and the streak continues, as I just can't bring myself to cut corners on my health and balance.

FUELING WITH PURPOSE

Let's talk about what we are ingesting. If we want to have a strong and healthy body, we have to fuel it appropriately and this starts with keeping it hydrated and full of healthy, well-balanced food. This can be a challenge as you are always on the go as a principal. Many days, you are already running full speed before you even hit the front doors of the building, and you don't stop until the wee hours of the night. Many of us can be found walking the hallways, in classrooms, or in meetings with a full cup of coffee, a Diet Coke, or some other form of caffeine. How common is it that we guzzle water like we do caffeinated beverages? Hopefully it is starting to become more commonplace, but most often, it is not. The easiest way to get going with the water-drinking routine is to start carrying a water bottle with you to all your meetings. Make sure it has a grip-able lid or handle on it so you can carry it with ease. If you are in an old building and the water tastes like rusted pipes, invest in a water cooler or filtered water station for your building. Guaranteed the water consumption of your staff will triple! If water isn't easily accessible many of us won't seek it out. So, make it so easy that you can't *not* drink it.

Maybe you are like some of us who are stress eaters. When things hit the fan, if we aren't chewing gum, we are shoveling food into our mouths to help self-soothe all the stress and unrest around us. Hello, COVID! While this may have an immediate calming effect, it has a long-term impact on whether we can fit into our pants as the year progresses. Whatever is easily accessible in those stressful moments is what gets eaten—or inhaled. To combat this knee jerk reaction, especially if it's the staff-room goodies or the secretary's candy dish, have a plan. We have started to be intentional with what food we have on hand and visible to us throughout the school day. We purposefully put fruits and vegetables on our desks next to our computer monitors so we can just reach over and grab them when hit with a stress reaction. We also keep portion-packed almonds in our drawers. Premade protein shakes and spa water with lemons and cucumbers have also been super handy to help us keep to our plan. Making sure you are eating and drinking during the workday and that your choices are healthy is critical to maintaining a balanced lifestyle.

Take a moment and jot down a few healthy snacks that you can pack each day:

1.
2.
3.
4.

CONQUERING YOUR SCHEDULE

As you brainstorm possible ways to get your body moving, determining healthy snacks you can eat, and other things you can do to help create balance in your life, we encourage you to look at your daily schedule. Speakers Danny Bauer and Jessica Cabeen have written insightful blogs on conquering your schedule so it doesn't conquer you. Check them out! They share that you need to create structure within your day, sometimes even down to the detail of when you are going to spend time with your family, shower during quarantine, or exercise.

Thinking along the lines of your schedule and quarantine, many of us have found ourselves working longer and harder than we ever imagined possible since the spring of 2020, when we quickly shifted to virtual and distance learning across the nation. The long hours we were originally putting in at the building were now extended and blurred into the hours we spent at home with our families. To keep your home life and work life separate, we encourage you to set boundaries. We know for those of us who are workaholics, it can be hard to set them, and to keep them. Think about setting office hours. Reflect on how you are going to structure your day for maximum balance while still getting your job completed. Some leaders would commit themselves to always working out in the morning or evening, or to limiting the times they check emails throughout the day. Others would be clear about the times they were shutting off their email and not working, so they could spend time being present with their families or attending to self-care. Grab your calendar, and let's get scheduled.

ACCOUNTABILITY PARTNERS

We know and understand that finding balance can be a challenge. While many of us can take on these challenges alone and find success, others might appreciate and do better with an accountability partner. This is someone who can help remind us of our commitments when we begin working outside of the hours we set for ourselves, or when we are about to shove a third donut into our mouth. Having positive, encouraging support helps all of us stay focused, accountable, and goal-oriented. Over the years, we have enlisted our spouses, friends, fellow administrators, and colleagues as accountability partners. They may be on the same journey as us, or they may be on the sidelines, reminding us of the path and being our main cheerleaders. Seek out the support you need to help develop more long-term habits.

TURNING IT OFF

As much as we find ourselves eating, breathing, and living our job twenty-four hours a day, it is vital that we find turn it off. That's right: activate your automatic out-of-office email response and take a break. This means shutting your phone off and steering clear of social media. Use the "do not disturb" feature on your device and commit to going to that 5:30 spin class so you leave the office. Many of us struggle to find solutions to our challenges. We sometimes think that the more time we spend researching and trying to figure out an issue, the faster the solution will appear. Actually, when we turn off all the noise buzzing around us and relax, the solutions often magically emerge. Whether you turn off on vacation, on the weekend, or each night, you have to find a way to take a break. In fact, we encourage you to take advantage of the breaks built within the school year. Make sure to take time for yourself during winter break, spring break, or another time off from school. Often, we view these breaks as being just for teachers or students, when in fact, we need to start looking at how we can use them for ourselves. Each season of the school year has its own unique stresses and challenges, so take advantage of time without students and staff to recharge your battery so you can be strong for your community.

Not only is it healthy for you personally to have balance, it is also important to model the practice and communicate your approach to staff about the importance of self-care. When we continue to shove out emails and memos to staff during vacations and long past their contract hours, we send an unhealthy message to the people in our care. The three of us have found that the more we demonstrate self-care as a priority and keep balance at the forefront of our leadership, the healthier and happier our staff tends to be.

BE PRESENT

Finding balance is also about being fully present in whatever you are doing. Have you ever arrived in the parking lot at work and have no idea how you got there because you were so distracted? Yep, us too! We are also guilty of sitting across from someone and seeing their lips move but not "hearing" a word they said, because we were distracted by another situation. There will be seasons that are busier than others, and there will be times when we are way out of balance and have difficulty focusing. Acknowledge it. Own it. Get better.

Brainstorm some strategies that will help you stay present. For example, when you finally shut it down on the weekend, and it is your time to go for a run or walk, stop checking your email and social media feeds throughout your time on the road. Think about leaving your phone or computer in the trunk of your car for the first two hours after you get home. Suggest that all family members deposit their phones into a basket before going to the dinner table, and watch the conversation soar. Even writing a sticky on your laptop to say "Be Present" might be the reminder you need to stay focused on the person in front of you. Whatever it is, we encourage you to prevent distractions from taking away time you spend taking care of yourself or engaging with your friends and family. It is our belief that this time is precious and something we can't get back, so turn off the day and be fully present.

CHECKING YOUR STRESS LEVEL

Each of us has a high intensity job. Teachers, principals, vice principals, directors—you name it, all feel pressure. In fact, stress is one of the constants you can expect in life. There seems to always be something to worry about, even when life is going the right way. If we know stress is a constant, and we come to expect it, then it is something we can proactively address. While some folks might enjoy more vigorous exercise, as noted above, others might find yoga or meditation a better fit for them. Whatever it is, find a way to hold your stress at bay. We suggest you take a moment to identify and examine the causes of tension in your life. As you think through all the things that bring you stress, ponder the ways you can minimize or manage them. For example, cleaning the house after a hectic week is often the last thing that we want to do. Is there someone you can hire or bring in to help with this on a biweekly or monthly basis? Perhaps cooking meals stresses you out since you don't like to cook. Are there healthy meal kit services you could sign up for? Perhaps something at work is getting to you. Is there someone on staff who can help problem-solve or support you in addressing this area? The possibilities are endless as you start to identify and lessen your stressors.

FOSTERING RELATIONSHIPS

Think about how your relationships create balance in your life. Surrounding yourself with positive, healthy, and supportive people is critical to keeping this equilibrium. This includes both in your personal and professional lives. If someone is sucking the joy out of you, spewing negativity, or isn't adding value to your life you might need to reexamine the time you are spending with them, or consider ways to make the relationship more productive and positive. Nurturing relationships takes time and effort, but makes a significant impact on your overall wellbeing. We all need that person (or people) who listens and nods while you are pouring out your soul, hugs you tight, sends you a funny meme, has a cold beer and a bubble bath ready when you walk through the door, leaves you a note to say, "I believe in you," or shows up to Zoom calls with a ridiculous Snapchat filter just to make you laugh. Are you thinking of "your people"? We bet you are smiling. Identify the people who feed your soul and leave you feeling refreshed and energized. True relationships are ones that will help balance you out when times are crazy and will help pick you up when you are down. As you plan time for balance, make sure to include time to nurture these relationships with others.

You are important, and you need to invest in yourself. Take time out of each day to care for yourself, so you can bring your best self to your building and thrive while serving your community and students. If you don't take care of yourself, you can't effectively take care of others. After years of functioning at toxic levels, your life may start to unravel. Your health will deteriorate, your friendships and relationships will begin to fragment, and the quality of your work will decline. Start making changes today that will greatly impact the future. You are worth it.

> If you don't take care of yourself, you can't effectively take care of others.

INVITATION TO IMPLEMENT

You are important! Identify how you are going to move yourself up on your priority list:

- Look to your schedule. Where can you carve out time just for you on a daily basis?
- If you are struggling to find time, we encourage you to get up an hour earlier to exercise, meditate, read, journal, or connect with others.
- Set boundaries by creating a schedule for work and home hours—and stick with it.
- Say no.

Take care of your health! Make a plan for dialing in eating, sleep, and exercise!

- As you are thinking about your eating:
  - Remember to eat and hydrate regularly. Schedule it!
  - Have meals prepped and planned ahead of time.
  - Have healthy snacks available for your most vulnerable times.

- ○ Create a schedule for when you will be taking your nourishment breaks.
- ○ Connect with others during meals, whether that is in the lunch room or at the family dinner table.
- As you are thinking about your sleep:
  - ○ Find your optimal number of sleep hours.
  - ○ Don't overcommit, either with work or social events, to keep from eating into your sleep schedule.
  - ○ Reduce screen time before going to bed.
  - ○ Make your bedroom your technology free zone. Leave your devices in another room.
- As you are thinking about exercise:
  - ○ Find something that works for you, whether it is walking, yoga, CrossFit, or weight lifting.
  - ○ Think about how you can incorporate movement throughout your day such as visiting classrooms, playing tetherball at recess, or scheduling a virtual meeting to coincide with a walk.
  - ○ Just start, get going, and build momentum.

CHAPTER TWELVE

SHOW GRATITUDE AND GRACE

"Gratitude makes sense of our past, brings peace for today, and creates a vision for tomorrow."

—Melody Beattie

*A*n email from your boss flashes across your desk top: The Results Are In! Four weeks ago, your district sent out a survey to parents, and you are finally getting the results. You can't wait to dig into the data to see what your parents really think of your school. You flip through the report and are pleased to see higher-than-average marks in school communication, academic rigor, and safety. Your school has really been working hard in those areas, and you are thrilled to see that your parent community has noticed. You turn to the next page, which shows all the data on school culture. You scan down to the question that reads "Is the principal approachable?" Your finger travels to the percentages. *WHAT?!? Only 70 percent of my parents think I am approachable?* Ouch! How can that be? About that time, your counselor comes into your office. She sees the look on your face and asks, "What's wrong?" You explain that you received the parent survey results back. She asks, "How were they?" You sigh and say, "Awful! I can't believe that 30 percent of the parents think I'm unapproachable." You do not tell your colleague all the positive things in the report. The positives immediately vanished from your mind once you read that one unflattering percentage rate. For the next few weeks, you perseverate on that single piece of information and can't get it off your mind.

"Instead of focusing on the 5 percent, start by looking at the 95 percent." These are wise words Jessica Cabeen shared in her recent book, *Lead with Grace.* As a leader, it is easy to get sidetracked or fixated on the three staff members who don't support you, or on the work you are trying to do that is floundering. It is easy to focus on the two negative comments made in your latest survey, or to fixate on the teachers or parents who are always complaining. We get it. We strive for perfection. We all want our teams moving in the same direction, and it is frustrating when they don't. Leading with grace and gratitude is an important part of our practice, and it is all about shifting how you approach these issues in your day-to-day interactions. You are going to have challenges, sure you are going to mess up, and you might not ever have 100 percent of your team on board; but you can still lead with grace and gratitude. This mind-set will shift your entire view and experience of these events.

> Leading with grace and gratitude is an important part of our practice, and it is all about shifting how you approach these issues in your day-to-day interactions.

So, how do you lead with grace and gratitude? It starts with how you kick off your day. When your feet hit the ground in the morning, are you leading with appreciation? Do you take some time for yourself during these precious first few hours to get your head focused on what's most important? We have found journaling, reading, and reflecting help center us.

————————————— Rachael —————————————

A big part of my morning routine is to focus on gratitude and things I am thankful for. Each day, after I wake up and go for my morning run, I sit down with my coffee and write out ten things I am thankful for. While this is a great first step, I take it further by emailing, texting, or writing a note of appreciation to five people. By focusing on the positives and the things I am grateful for, it helps set my mind on a positive path for the rest of the day.

This approach to gratitude carries itself into the workday in a variety of ways. In their book Lead like a PIRATE, Shelley Burgess and Beth Houf wrote about dropping "anchors of appreciation," which is a consistent practice in my building. Each week, I work to make a conscious and consistent effort to reach out and share my appreciation with those are around me. I explicitly identify what I am grateful for and note how it connects to the work we are doing as a building. I drop these anchors of appreciation as I move throughout the building and from classroom to classroom. Sometimes I use anchor-themed notepaper, while other times I use sticky notes or signature notepads with a cute emoji and font. Regardless, I always try to find a way to celebrate those around me.

While it's great for us to acknowledge those around us, as leaders we are constantly working to amplify this mindset of appreciation among our staff. One thing Kate uses in her school is "notes of appreciation." During the week, staff members fill out gratitude slips for their colleagues and put them in a box in the work room. At the beginning or end of staff meetings, Kate will read off a few of these notes. She also always includes "Kudos from Kate" in her weekly bulletin. This is such a great practice that Rachael picked it up and started doing it a few years back. Just like Kate said would happen, people started posting those notes of appreciation in their workspaces and focusing more on showing gratitude to others. Talk about a simple way to increase positive culture.

We've shared a number of ways you can embed gratitude into your day. We know there are lots of other ideas out there. Take a moment and write down some ways you could envision gratitude and appreciation as part of your daily routine

1.	
2.	
3.	
4.	
5.	

Kourtney

Carol Dweck's growth mindset work was one of the things that transformed my building. A shift to the belief that the intelligence and capacity of each individual in the system is unknown and unlimited was exactly what we needed. This work changed our view from an insurmountable mountain of problems to solve, to a growth model where the prospects were limitless. The potential for change when you are suddenly living in the possibilities is so energizing.

Instead of dwelling on a deficit model, growth mindset helped us focus on the positive, live in the light, embrace challenge, and seek to learn to see mistakes as opportunities. Basically, it taught us to give grace to ourselves when we stumbled with our imperfections and share grace with each other as we traveled this road together.

An amazing thing happens when you make this shift in mindset: by investing more energy in seeing positivity, the heaviness of the work lessens. Instead of stumbling through my days, complaining about how hard it was and seeing the obstacles as negatives, I was answering a call to action with gratitude leading the charge

It is really easy to think of growth mindset as being something that is rolled out with kids. The reality is that is sooooooo much more about the grownups than the children. Growth mindset guru Kendra Coates once suggested to me that it's not about checking the growth-mindset box like, "Okay, I read that and have it now"; it's more like a ball you hold throughout the day, one that we sometimes drop and need to pick up again.

Leading with gratitude as an administrator helps you stay in a growth mindset. In each demanding situation, looking for the positive, seeking out the challenge, and striving toward the possibility helps you constantly seek growth. It also helps you stay connected to the people around you, to be the authentic boots-on-the-ground leader who inspires change with grace and style.

SHOW GRACE

Showing and expressing gratitude is the gateway to leading with grace. When we focus on the positives and are grounded within ourselves, it is much easier to lead with grace. In fact, in moments where we find it hard to lead with dignity, it often is connected to our lack of gratitude and appreciation for others. Leading with grace isn't about what you say, or how you say it or how you respond to others. It truly comes down to soft skills.

For many of us, leading with grace is not something they taught in principal school. Sure, they talked about leadership, but not the soft skills that were needed to build culture, relationships, and turn a building around while empowering teachers. Through trial and error, we have found that leading with kindness is a must. We must have grace with ourselves and with others as we work together to change the trajectory for students.

For starters, we need to understand that we aren't perfect, and we are going to make mistakes. Sure, none of us likes to mess up, but it is inevitable: failure is part of the growth process. Instead of fixating on our mistakes or shortcomings, we need to give ourselves permission to make mistakes and learn from them. If we are always trying to play it safe and be perfect, our personal and professional growth will be at a snail's pace, and we don't have time for that. So, in an effort to assist with this growth, you need to be vulnerable.

> We must have grace with ourselves and with others as we work together to change the trajectory for students.

Sometimes as leaders we find ourselves putting up professional walls between us and our staff. Perhaps this might look like withholding personal details about yourself with your staff or not expressing emotions when they arise. Holding back might make things appear easier on the surface. However, the lack of connection and depth you'll have in your staff relationships will become significantly more apparent when you are faced with challenging times. After all, relationships aren't built during times of challenge or conflict, they are tested. Relationships are best cultivated and created in the months and years leading up to the conflict. An authentic relationship is developed by being vulnerable, honest, and transparent. This starts with how leaders approach daily staff interactions and the layers of themselves they choose to share. This can be a delicate balance. We don't want to spew negativity every time we come up against adversity, either personally or professionally, but you do need to give yourself permission to let staff know when you are having a hard day or need support. If you communicate when you are hurting or struggling, you'll find staff will be much more open to sharing with you. We know this can be scary to do if you haven't ventured into this arena before, but it is truly worth it.

ADMIT WHEN YOU ARE WRONG

Part of being vulnerable is admitting when we are wrong. We all mess up. We all make mistakes. Instead of hiding these moments, embrace them and have a conversation with the person or group that it impacted. We recommend you acknowledge your errors and faults in person whenever possible. The authenticity of the conversation is so much deeper and transparent than if an email is sent or the conversation occurs over the phone, where you can't see the other person's reaction. If the blunder, misunderstanding, or oversight impacted a large group of people, put on the extra deodorant, take a few deep breaths, and call them together for a meeting. When you apologize, being able to admit you are wrong to those you lead is an incredible display of grace and strength.

SAY YOU ARE SORRY

"I am sorry." Sharing these three magic words shows an incredible display of grace. These words are extremely powerful and are often not uttered by leaders when they should be. Call it pride. Call it insecurity. Whatever it is, it's not leading with honor and authenticity when a leader can't apologize for their actions or inaction. Sometimes we unintentionally hurt people's feelings. Other times we say things that we shouldn't when our filter slips at that exact moment, and what should have remained in your head comes barreling out of our mouth. As we learn and grow, mistakes will be made, and many of these will impact others. Apologizing mends wounds, shows vulnerability, and models the kind of behavior we want to see in both our students and our staff. It takes grace to realize when these moments have occurred and to respond appropriately by saying you are sorry and that you'll learn and grow from the experience.

GIVE YOURSELF GRACE

Many of us have perfectionist tendencies along with a need for control. We get it. We are right there with you. A challenge we are often faced with is when we believe we have fallen short of perfection or have disappointed others. This is honestly the worst feeling. The drop in your stomach. The increased heart rate. The sweaty palms and the thoughts swirling in your mind that you should have done something differently.

We all hate it when we mess up, but it is inevitable. As we personally grow in our practice, we have to be okay with not being perfect and accepting failures. Isn't it ironic that we preach a growth mindset with our students and teachers, but it is sometimes so challenging to accept for ourselves? So, stop beating yourself up and fixating on the mistakes. Embrace your blunders and have the grace with yourself to understand you are a work in progress.

UNDERSTAND PEOPLE

You need to understand yourself in order to understand others. While this seems easy on the surface, knowing yourself and how you interact with others can be a significant challenge, as you have to be honest with how you respond in moments when you aren't necessarily your best self. However, once you gain this awareness, the opportunities are endless in understanding others. The book *Reading People: How Seeing the World through the Lens of Personality Changes Everything* by blogger and podcaster Anne Bogel has been instrumental in helping us understand and make sense of our interactions with others. As we work to deepen this knowledge, it has helped us better serve those we lead by demonstrating that we see them as individuals, that we care for them, and that we support them in their work. It has also helped with our awareness of why people act the way they do, without making inaccurate assumptions about them, particularly if their responses are different from what we would do. Taking this a step further, understanding people also helps you to realize that a person's behavior has more to do with their own internal struggles than it ever did with you. Through this, you learn and lead with grace.

> You need to understand yourself in order to understand others.

LET'S GET GRITTY

Now that we have covered the warm fuzzy topics of grace and gratitude, we are going to catapult into the arena of grit and perseverance. The word grit conjures up images of weathered faces, dirty fingernails, clenched teeth, and dripping sweat. Although, not much different than what you might look like after recess duty or chaperoning a middle school dance, grit does go beyond physical appearance to a deep-rooted fire in your belly that radiates determination and resiliency.

For her book *Grit*, psychologist Angela Duckworth completed an extensive study on common traits that successful people hold. One clear trait that rose to the surface was grit. She explains that grit is a combination of passion and perseverance for a singularly important goal. Before Duckworth made "grit" an educational buzzword, many of us would have described this invaluable trait as the persistent determination of never giving up, no matter how tough the situation. We show it in our tireless work ethic and our laser-focused diligence to succeed.

This fire developed early for many of us and accompanied us on our journeys as youths. It may have been there when we finished the last mile in our cross-country races, carried us through trying out for the school musical, and maybe even developed in our quest for someone's affection. As young adults, we persisted as we completed the late-night essay to get into our dream college, and as we paraded across that graduation stage several years later. It forced us to ignore the rejection letters and apply just one more time for our first job. Tenacity also allowed us to persist through life's hard lessons, like the fourteen-hour days during our first year of teaching, and it gave us the shovels to dig deeper when we received our first humbling mark on our evaluation. Our determination insisted that we complete our administration programs while balancing a full-time job, multiple kids, and an ailing parent. Now we are turning, once again, to tenacity, perseverance, and grit in our leadership roles.

We will all make mistakes, render unpopular decisions, and utterly and completely fail. There will be yelling parents, grievances filed, and phone calls to the board of directors. These things will hurt our feelings, bring on choking sobs, and make us feel inadequate and defeated. They may even make us question our chosen profession. There will be days when we want to hide under the bedcovers, we are so steeped with anxiety, doubt, frustration, or anger. And when you are at your lowest point, willpower will swoop in and give you a stern talking to, slap you upside your head, and help you put one foot in front of the other.

We all know people who are strong and weather even the most formidable experiences. They tackle grim challenges with bravery and grace. Their shield of valor shows in their resilience and perseverance as the waves of stress and disagreement crash into them. Do you ever wonder how some people can carry such burdens, and others of us are left debilitated?

Adding tenacity, perseverance, and grit to your wheelhouse is a journey. Unfortunately, in order to acquire these traits, leaders must dance with adversity. Each unsavory experience allows us to practice how to navigate the situation and builds our muscles of courage. Pause and think about your last tough situation:

- How did you gather information to understand the circumstances?
- What part did you play in the situation?
- How did your response either help or harm?
- How did you use your mentors and network to gather resources needed to solve the problem?
- How did you take care of yourselves at the conclusion?

We know that writing things down helps us process, so think about having a "grit journal" where you keep track of difficult experiences. Over time, you can analyze your experiences and determine trends and growth. Switch your mindset from allowing negative experiences to tear you down to using these experiences as building blocks to resiliency.

Kate

Twenty-seven students in my self-contained behavior class whose actions left me questioning my ability to protect my students and staff at any given moment. Budget cuts that left us with a skeleton crew. An overnight change in our student population that left me pondering my middle-class biases. Oh, and then there was the throbbing pressure of making the state's adequate yearly progress, which resulted in having our scores displayed on the front page of the newspaper.

This all left me defeated, weary, and susceptible to shingles three times in one year. There were days I wanted to walk away and questioned if I was the right person for the job. I felt like I was on a treadmill that was turned up way beyond my capacity, running furiously, but staying in the same place. And yet if I stopped running, I would be thrown off the track and catapulted into a wall. As I was crashing, the deep, baritone voice of Grit radiated in my head. This was the same voice that had told me several years before to get up and ski down a mountain after severing my ACL. This voice was telling me to dig deep, get up, don't be a wimp, and persevere.

So, I did. I stared adversity in the eye and slowly took back control. I leaned heavily on the support of colleagues, friends, and family. You cannot be an island and expect to survive. I recognized that I needed to be brave enough to show my vulnerability and admit that I needed help. The fear of failing was leaving me paralyzed, and I needed to regain my own power.

I wiped the self-pity and tears away and embraced a good dose of honest feedback and fresh perspectives. I recognized that I was a sensitive person whose feelings were easily hurt. I therefore had to toughen up and not take things so personally. The days that had been filled with haphazard, reactive actions eventually gave way to systematic protocols that anticipated hardship. Tough conversations led to enlightenment. Mistakes turned into growth opportunities filled with optimism, and defeating moments led to courageous confidence. If you find yourself in a situation of despair, flip your mindset. Be vulnerable, seek advice, proactively create a plan, and take control of your own destiny.

INVITATION TO IMPLEMENT

- Leading with gratitude will change a school's culture. Embed gratitude into your daily practice!
- How can you extend grace to those around you? Create a game plan for incorporating this into your leadership.
- Grit and resilience are key to the principalship. Identify how you can reflect on and learn from challenging experiences.

CONCLUSION: LEAD WITH LOVE

"Love isn't a state of perfect caring. It is an active noun. To love someone is to strive to accept that person exactly the way he or she is, right here and now."

–Fred Rogers

This morning seems like an eternity ago when you pull into the empty parking lot, absent of any life except the song of an early bird. The wind is gnawing at your back as you fumble for your keys, hoping that Alzheimer's hasn't completely invaded your brain as you try to remember the code to the alarm. As the teakettle boils, you peruse your to-do list from yesterday. A flicker of disappointment strikes you because you only crossed off one item on that extensive list, even though you came home with rings of sweat on your shirt from the toil of the day. "Today will be different," you muse to yourself, and you optimistically dive into your day, determined to make an impact on your community.

How can you, as the leader of hundreds of students and dozens of staff members, make the biggest impact? Looming thoughts of the upcoming statewide assessment swirl in your brain, and you question if your standards for your staff and students have been rigorous enough to meet demanding benchmarks. Then, the pendulum in your mind

swings, and you smile as you remember the three fourth-grade girls in your office painting fingernails last Friday. On the surface, one might think, "Why in the world is that principal painting fingernails when those girls should be in reading groups?" You know why. You know that one of the students with freshly lacquered nails was recently removed from her parents by child services, and she was steeped in grief. You know that she had been isolating herself from her friends and hadn't turned in any assignments to her teacher in weeks. You *know* that it was worth the time away from academics to paint fingernails with her pals because she needed a little joy in her life. Some would argue that painting fingernails wasn't going to help her pass the state assessment. We think otherwise. Assessing the whole child by matching our interventions to their needs is essential. We should attune our actions to our students' emotional and social well-being all while removing obstacles that hinder academic progress. This might mean that some days a child may not be ready for learning academics and instead needs us to foster a place for physical and emotional security. As Kristin Van Marter Souers and Pete Hall so wisely shared in their book *Relationship, Responsibility and Regulation*, it is all about creating a safe nest for students so that they can learn, thrive, and soar.

We want students and staff to achieve, but still love and find joy with learning. We want to push students and staff to new heights, but still have them make deep connections with their community. We want students and staff to challenge and explore new ideas, but still remain respectful and thoughtful. We want students and staff to hit all the necessary benchmarks, but show creativity and bravery. We want students and staff to blaze new pathways, but be inclusive and accepting. We want students and staff to be productive and show perseverance, but be emotionally grounded. We want to impact all of these things for our students and staff, but do we have the capacity, the knowledge, the energy . . . and enough Snickers bars to achieve it all?

As we look through these *wants*, one word stands out for us. It is the term *but*. Kate's father (a past superintendent of schools) would say that "but" is the great eraser word. He would quip, "Anything before the conjunction *but* might as well have not been said at all, because *but* negates anything that precedes it." So, ask yourself: If we want students and staff to achieve, can we simultaneously instill rigor *and* love? Many educators and researchers would embrace the "but" and say there is no possible way that schools could reach high achievement while still infusing love and joy. We would like to challenge that thinking and swipe that pendulum right off its pivot. We believe that educational leaders can have fun with their community, and greet students and staff every day with hugs, laughter, humor, and connection, and still hold them to rigorous academic and behavioral standards. You don't have to choose. In fact, we are so thoroughly committed to love that we don't think you can have a well-balanced and healthy culture if you are not committed to love.

Rachael

How can I come at this conversation from a place of love? This was the critical question I was asking myself as I headed into a meeting with a staff member whom I was really irritated with. The frustration—and anger—had emerged because I wasn't happy with how a particular situation was handled, and that a student had been held responsible for the teacher's challenges. We were blaming students instead of looking to ourselves for how we could all improve. The challenging part was that I knew if I went into the conversation with this chip on my shoulder, the situation would only blow up, and could possibly turn catastrophic. I knew it could potentially damage the relationship I had with the staff member and also impact the steps they were taking to get better. Again, my question was: How could I come at this conversation from a place of love?

When the staff member came into my office for the meeting, I made sure my body position was open and that I sat next to them in the room. I started off by affirming my beliefs about the teacher, and how they were incredible at their craft. I used this entry point to shift into asking how they were doing, as the situation at hand was something that was not in alignment with what I knew to be true about them and their heart. I expressed my care and concern that they feel happy, supported, and effective. Once I did that, I sat quietly as I waited for them to respond. In time, the teacher started sharing things that were going on outside of the classroom, things at home and in their personal life that were impacting their work. They said that they were trying to work on things and that they were trying to keep it all together; however, it wasn't always possible.

After the teacher spoke, I asked clarifying questions and asked how I could support them. We made some plans to help, both in and out of the classroom, which we would frequently check in about in the coming months. As I reflect back on this conversation, it could have gone a multitude of ways. I could have been the jerk principal who doesn't care and just comes in and lets people have it. Instead, I came at it with love and care and sought to support the teacher. This simple change made all the difference in the world.

So, what does love got to do with it? (Go ahead, start singing with Tina Turner.) Love is belonging, and when people feel they belong, they will generally behave and perform positively. We know there are educators who are uncomfortable with using the word "love" in association with our students and staff. It is a strong concept that holds a tremendous amount of power. Some may think that bringing love into a school setting crosses a professional boundary and is inappropriate to say. There are those who may have a difficult time expressing love to family and friends, let alone to students and staff. However, no matter your situation, we are all in positions where we have the privilege to show we truly love the people in our care, it just may look different for various educators. Love does make the world go 'round and we think it *does* belong in our schools.

There are many ways to show your love. Some are more outward, while others are quiet acts. Some of us may be comfortable saying "I love you!" over the intercom, or as we are high-fiving students as they stream down the hallway. Others of us may *show* our love by giving extra tutoring to students after school or donating money to an account so a child can eat lunch. Love can also be shown by writing postcards or making phone calls to share a student's triumphs, or it may come in the form of noticing a student is absent from school, driving to their apartment, and insisting that you love them enough to get them out of bed and to school.

Show your love for your community so deeply that you set your expectations high and hold your community accountable. Encourage perseverance and growth. Many of us are guilty of saving our students from struggling, and this can result in learned helplessness. Create a culture of learning that honors productive struggle. Ask yourself who is the hardest working person in the room. It should be the students, not the teachers. If we are always "saving" our students from discomfort, they will never reach their potential. Love them enough to engage them in higher-order thinking. Encourage them to take risks and solve problems in multiple ways. Invite them to form partnerships with others so they can negotiate, empathize, and collaborate.

Love your students enough that you differentiate your management techniques, and hold people accountable while striving to understand the "why" behind the behavior. We know that problem-solving in the heat of the moment is not productive, so you may allow an unsavory word or action to slide. However, it is imperative that we follow up after the person has de-escalated. If we allow unproductive behavior to live in our environment, it will grow and take over our culture. Allowing our students to roam the hallways for hours or cuss out one of our professionals without follow through only breeds more problems. Our job is to prepare our students for the future, and that includes having high expectations for behavior. There are many culturally and trauma-informed practices to coach our students to regulated behavior. Research up and implement those lofty behavior expectations.

We have an incredible opportunity before us. We have been given the honor to positively impact our students through growing and supporting them in academics, attitudes, and attendance, all while building meaningful relationships. Your staff deserves to be nurtured and held in the highest regard, as you push them to investigate research, differentiate instruction, and productively and relentlessly engage their students. While this all sounds grand and wonderful in theory, there will be hiccups. We know there will come a time where you will be tested and tried. You will feel tired and wonder if your work is making a difference. During moments of despair, we encourage you to respond with love. It is easy to throw in the towel or settle for average, but we can't be swayed in our commitment to cultivating a positive path for both our staff and students' futures. We must strive for excellence, and we must respond with love.

Kourtney

Mother Theresa wisely said, "I have found the great paradox, that if you love until it hurts, there can be no more hurt, only more love." Educators who love deeply are my favorite. Nothing is more powerful than a teacher connecting with a student, meeting their eyes, and saying, "I care too much to let you fail." That "we've got this" relationships move mountains.

In my building, we had a lot of students who had more adverse childhood experiences than years. There is one special one who had a range of obstacles, including an incarcerated father, living with a mother who struggled with mental illness, physical abuse from Mom's boyfriend, exposure to drugs, bouts of homelessness, and child protection involvement. The staff wrapped their arms around this family, and I mean tightly. Things like secretaries letting him in early in the morning when he was dropped off before dawn; our counselor hooking him up with community mental health services at school so he wouldn't need to be absent; our homeless liaison arranging for transportation so he could stay at our school while his family was couch surfing; support staff organizing supplies from our food pantry to send home on weekends; teachers joining me on home visits to connect with the family and identify additional needs. All of these things so that school could be the steady, calm, predictable place for this child. When I think about this student, it would have been so easy for the team to say, "You know what, this kid has enough going on, let's lessen the academic demands for a while." But you know what? They didn't. They met the child's eyes with their own and said, "I've got you. You can do this. I'm here to help you."

After experiencing three years of instability, last year he was in third grade and took the state assessments for the first time. This child exceeded in ELA and in math. Was this his most important accomplishment? No. But of the barriers this child will experience, a solid academic foundation will not be one of them. The doors of the future are open to this sweet kid because this team of teachers loved him, believed in him, and were relentless in their support.

Leading with love is just as critical as an administrator. Love sets the "why" firmly in place. We are doing this work because we love our kids too much to allow them to fail. We are supporting each other because we care too much about this team to let any one person stumble. If you were to ask my staff if I pushed them to perform better, I'm pretty confident they would say "Absolutely," but more importantly I hope they would also say that they felt deeply cared about.

A team that feels loved and appreciated will rise beyond expectations. We know the connection between student-teacher relationships and student achievement, but somehow in our field, we tend not to see how this same phenomenon translates between staff and administrators. Do you think administrators are afraid to show deep love and appreciation? Sometimes I wonder. It requires vulnerability, and that can feel risky. I think it is worth the risk. In fact, I've never seen a school community that rises without it.

Love. Love big enough to hold the high expectations, have the hard conversations, give the important feedback, and be relentless in the support of your team. Love them so much you won't let them fail.

Love your staff enough to set the bar high. Whether it is creating a protocol to follow up with staff goal-setting, or leading with the expectation that everyone arrive to work on time, or insisting your staff have their lesson plans completed before the start of the week. Love your staff enough to notice their struggles *and* their accomplishments. Celebrate with your staff when they have taken risks, made improvements, and diligently persevered. Care enough to inspect what you expect and have productive conversations when staff members are faltering. Love may shine brightly by covering a teacher's class so they can go to their own child's music performance, or by allowing them to leave early to get to a doctor's appointment. Give them permission to take a mental health day when you know they won't take it themselves. Tend to your staff's concerns and listen to their worries, but love them enough to not solve their problems for them. Instead, help them tackle their own hardships, with you as their confidant and cheerleader. Follow through with promises and admit when you are wrong. All of these actions equate to love.

> Love your students and staff enough to get to know them so you can lead your community to greatness.

Love your students and staff enough to get to know them so you can lead your community to greatness. The most powerful way to know your community is to be visible. Strive to be the person whom people truly know in your community. One of the greatest compliments is when your students are able to introduce you to their parents by name. We know this may be a small thing, but this gesture means that they recognize your face and your name and feel connected enough to you that they want to share you with their parents.

Love your community enough to vulnerably learn, listen, and grow. We all work with communities that distinguish themselves in their own way. The composition of our communities is uniquely created by diverse personalities, races, socioeconomic status, cultures, and many other attributes. And into our communities, we bring our own biases and assumptions. As leaders, you have the opportunity to learn and grow with your distinctive community and to ponder the circumstances that its individuals experience. While we will never truly completely understand what it's like to be another person, widening your perspectives, building your knowledge, and refining your understanding are part of the growth process for leaders.

Often, leaders are so busy making assumptions that they don't look beyond their institutional walls to find the real meaning behind the personality, the outburst, the failing score, and the attendance percentage. Love your school community enough go below the surface and recognize the "why" behind the actions. We think this will add to your credibility and success.

Below are some example statements that may bring meaning to the actions of students. We encourage you to add a few other statements after reflecting on your own community:

- We have students whose only predictable meal comes from what we serve at school.
- We have students who look forward to the positive connection they have with staff each day, as this is the only time they are told they are loved, cherished, and capable of incredible things.
- We have students who don't have consistent heat or air conditioning in their homes, so they are freezing or sweltering when school is not in session.
- We have students who have inconsistent family structures and may not be confident about who will be at home when they arrive after school.
- We have students who arrive home to an evening of being alone, because both parents work late into the night.
- We have students who are the primary caregivers to their younger siblings and don't have time to complete homework.
- We have students and families that don't have enough money to cover utilities, housing, and food.
- We have students who don't have healthy relationships with those outside of school, so they live in fear or unrest due to never knowing what might come next.
- We have staff who are going through divorces, caring for elderly parents, experiencing trauma, worried about paying the bills, or were just diagnosed with cancer.

All of these factors may result in students and staff being tired, cranky, unfocused, or withdrawn. They may result in students seeking negative attention, or showing obstinance and defiance. Perhaps it shows up in uncontrollable sobs, talking sharply to others, disengagement, or domineering control. In addition to outward signs of grief, worry, and anger, signs may also come in the forms of lack of hygiene, failure to follow through, or quiet isolation.

After pondering the circumstances of your students, staff and families, think about how you can react with love:

- Instead of getting frustrated when a student isn't remembering how to enter the school calmly, lovingly respond with reteaching a procedure.
- Instead of using a sharp tone with a student who doesn't understand the directions, respond by lovingly crouching beside them and privately repeating the directions step-by-step, or include a visual representation.
- Instead of becoming irritated that someone is throwing a tantrum *again*, invite that student to play a game with you at recess time and pump them full of loving praise.
- Instead of sending that scathing email to a parent about their child's disrespect, pause and instead ask questions of curiosity.
- Instead of becoming disappointed because staff aren't showing up to meetings on time, respond with a private check-in after school to find out the "why."
- Instead of beating yourself up for staff not meeting your expectations, respond by lovingly reworking norms, gathering feedback, and evaluating your clarity of communication.

Kate

I grew up in a family that said "I love you" all the time. We wouldn't leave the house without saying those three precious words. Phone conversations ended with the sentiment, not once, but often three or four times. We outwardly showed our affection by hugging often, sitting close on the couch, and linking arms on a walk. We inscribed hearts on steamy bathroom mirrors and left notes under pillows with lipstick-smudged imprints. Love came in sharing meals with neighbors, grocery shopping for homeless shelters, and delivering Mason jars of freshly canned peaches to brighten someone's day. Mom shared her love by teaching us how to cook, sew, and set an elegant table. She was the mom who always had a fresh batch of cookies and a cold soda waiting for the gaggle of friends who walked through the door after school. Dad showed his love by instilling in us his work ethic, integrity, and high standards. He pushed us to take risks and fill our schedule with one more math class. Although I lost both of them to cancer at an early age, their values of infusing love with high expectations have carried into my career.

I'll admit, throughout my career there have been people who have warned me about getting too close, drawing professional boundaries, taking the worry home with me, and being mindful of the risk of hugging students. While I do believe it is important to be professional, I also believe that one of the most important things you can do as a leader is to love the people in your care deeply while still having rigorous standards. This love can be shown through human connection and taking the time to know the stories of your students, staff, and families. It can shine through in the messaging on your school walls, and when you take the time to grow and learn with your community. So, go out there and show your love!

LOVE IS HUMAN CONNECTION

A loving culture starts and ends with human connection. We've all walked down hallways and passed by staff members we've worked with years who may never utter a greeting, let alone stop and check in with you. How many times have you entered a school, and the office staff barely lifts their heads to greet you? It leaves many of us feeling empty and rejected. One of the first steps in building a positive and loving culture is to set the standard that your staff needs to acknowledge each other, their students, and their community members and visitors. Start with declaring the expectation that whenever staff members walk past another human being, they have to make eye contact, smile, and say a minimum of "hello." We know this sounds simple, and some people will find it an odd request, but it is a critical step in modeling that connection is important to a positive culture. You'll be amazed at how many staff members, as well as visitors, notice and appreciate the positive interactions. This routine says, "I see you, and you are important."

IS YOUR SPACE COMMUNICATING LOVE?

We all know that spaces elicit feelings. A space can provide instant serenity and comfort, or stress, confusion, and anxiety, just by how it is organized, the lighting, the messaging that appears on the walls, and even how it smells. Have you paused and reflected on what your space is communicating to your community? Consider conducting a space audit in your building. This assessment can start with you, but we encourage you to invite others to give you feedback. When your community enters your school, your office, your sports fields, or even your parking lot, what do they see? What do they hear? What do they smell? What do they feel?

Your space is your first impression, and it is an important part of communicating your priorities and values. Are your posters in the hallways focused on including others, being kind, and persevering, or are they filled with signs that say, "don't do this" and "that is isn't allowed"? Is your space organized and updated with clear procedures, or are parents lost, confused, and overwhelmed when they enter? Do your bulletin boards, artwork, and displays reveal what is important in your school community? Do the items you choose for your office invite others into your life, or is your space void of the photographs and personal items? Take a whiff. Does it smell like bleach water and gym sweat, or cinnamon spice? An instant crowd-pleaser is aromatherapy via a plug-in air freshener or essential oil diffuser. Whether it is adding a table lamp, painting one wall a pretty shade of blue, or having candy in the middle of your table, grasp the invitation to make your space more appealing, inclusive, and welcoming. Your community will instantly notice the difference.

LOVE IS BEING VISIBLE

We all know that we could stay busy in our office with the door shut for eight hours every day. Resist the urge! One of the most important strategies that will improve almost every facet of your job is visibility. People need to see you. They need to know that you care enough to show up and see them in their environment. Whether it is popping by the kitchen to compliment the cook for creating the best wiener wraps in the county, or sitting down and listening to an English department plan lessons before school, or cheering on a kiddo at recess who wants to show off their four-square talents. You can show your love by being visible. Your students, staff, families, and volunteers need to know that what they are doing matters, and that they are important to you. Don't be the principal that everyone stops and stares at when entering a space because they are so unused to you being there. Your presence should be natural and expected. Strive to be so visible that people notice when you are gone. Be that person who is at the entrances hugging, high-fiving, (or foot-tapping and elbow-bumping during pandemics) and sharing loving sentiments not only to the children, but their family members. Be that person who knows every student's name. Be that person who knows their staff so well you can tell when they need support by just looking at them. You are a fabulous person, so allow your community to get to know you as you get to know them.

Love can be sprinkled in a thousand different ways. Your love will be reflected in the legacy you leave behind. Consider for a moment that the measure of your success is not in the daily grind of tasks, but in the relationships you cultivate, the belief you inspire in those around you, and the ways you empower others to make changes for our children. The strongest leaders do not put themselves at the center, but carefully coach from the side, knowing that this fosters sustainability for the greater community. When you care deeply, the people around you feel it, and it transforms the impact of your leadership. Every day you have the ability to transform the trajectory for the students in your building. Your impact is vast and incredibly important. Lead with vision. Focus on the important things. Have high expectations. And do all of these things with great love. Reece Witherspoon said, "You always gain by giving love." So, when you sit at your desk on that dark and chilly morning and you ask yourself, "What the heck am I doing in this profession?" you will think, I am infusing rigor and love into my community so that they will have optimal achievement and happiness for a bright future. After all, love makes the world go around.

Speaking of love . . . We love that you have taken time out of your incredibly busy life to read our book. Our goal in writing these chapters was to let you know you are not alone in this journey. We understand the complexity of your position, and sometimes it is nice to know that other leaders have similar struggles. We hope you have absorbed a few tips and strategies to help you navigate your world of leadership. While we know each of you has a unique style and is leading in a different situation , think about how you can capture a few of the strategies and approaches we discussed and make them your own.

Remember, you are not alone in this journey. Although most of us have never met in person, we are now connected. We'd love to be part of your network, so don't hesitate to contact us and/or visit our website. We are continually learning and growing, too, so please share how you creatively implemented an idea from our book, found a new way to circumvent an issue, or celebrated an accomplishment.

Although you may not hear it every day, we want you to know that you are appreciated and valued. Our wish for you is that you find the people who will support you, give you valuable feedback and help you grow. We want you to aspire to work through your strengths to optimize your potential. When you are clarifying your purpose, don't forget to authentically inspire others so you can collectively move in the same direction. Select those few goals that include core instruction, culture, and collaboration, and stay focused. Remember, competing pathways will try to lure you away. Stay strong and consistent. And please, don't forget the importance of balance and the power of love in your life. You are a hero to the students, staff, and families that you serve, and we applaud you.

INVITATION TO IMPLEMENT

Make a list of how you show love to the people in your care. Perhaps categorize how you show your love. Remember, one size does not fit all, so differentiate your actions.

Spoken words:

- Spoken words of praise at the beginning or end of your staff meetings.
- Starting a committee meeting with accolades
- In-the-moment authentic appreciation verbiage, for example, when you are introducing someone, share something about how much you value their work ethic, their connections with the students, or their contribution to a committee.

Written words:

- Notes of appreciation after you complete an observation or after you pop by a classroom.
- A handwritten note to share an encouraging word.
- Words of appreciation in a weekly bulletin.
- A formal letter placed in their personnel file.

Physical connections:

- High fives
- Fist bumps
- Hugs

Gifts of time, trinkets, and treats:

- Volunteering to cover someone's class so they can make an appointment.

- Putting together care kits for teachers who were catapulted into online learning during quarantine time.
- Providing coffee and donuts "just because."
- Wheeling around a cold beverage cart on a hot afternoon.
- High expectations with follow through for all—be equitable with all staff.
- Incorporate a system for identifying action items at the end of each meeting.
- If you say you are going to do something, do it!

RECOMMENDED RESOURCES

BOOKS

The 5 Languages of Appreciation in the Workplace: Empowering Organizations by Encouraging People by Gary Chapman and Paul White

140 Twitter Tips for Educators: Get Connected, Grow Your Professional Learning Network, and Reinvigorate Your Career by Brad Curry, Billy Krakower, and Scott Rocco

A Leader's Guide to Reflective Practice by Judy Brown

Culturize: Every Student. Every Day. Whatever it Takes by Jimmy Casas

Crucial Accountability: Tools for Resolving Violated Expectations, Broken Commitments, and Bad Behavior by Kerry Patterson, Joseph Grenny, David Maxfield, Ron McMillan, and Al Switzler

From Leading to Succeeding: The Seven Elements of Effective Leadership in Education by Douglas Reeves

Hard Conversations Unpacked: The Whos, the Whens, and the What-Ifs by Jennifer Abrams

Lead Like a PIRATE: Make School Amazing for Your Students and Staff by Shelley Burgess and Beth Houf

Lead with Grace: Leaning into the Soft Skills of Leadership by Jessica Cabeen

Leaders of Learning: How District, School, and Classroom Leaders Improve Student Achievement by Richard DuFour and Robert J. Marzano

Leading with Focus: Elevating the Essentials for School and District Improvement by Mike Schmoker

Lean In: Women, Work, and the Will to Lead by Sheryl Sandberg

Mindset: The New Psychology of Success, How We can Learn to Fulfill Our Potential by Carol S. Dweck

The Miracle Morning: The 6 Habits That Will Transform Your Life before 8 a.m. by Hal Elrod

Thanks for the Feedback: The Science and Art of Receiving Feedback Well by Douglas Stone and Sheila Henn

Visible Learning for Teachers: Maximizing Impact on Learning by John Hattie

PODCASTS AND LISTSERVS

ASCD Learn Teach Lead Radio
Better Leaders, Better Schools
Marshall Memo
ASCD SmartBrief
Teaching Keating with Weston and Molly Kieschnick
TED Talks Education
Transformative Principal with Jethro Jones
Master of Memory

TWITTER

Adam Welcome @mradamwelcome
Amber Teamann @8amber8
Amy Fast @fastcrayon
Andy Jacks @_AndyJacks

Baruti Kafele @PrincipalKafele
Beth Houf @BethHouf
Dave Burgess @burgessdave
Jessica Cabeen @JessicaCabeen
Jessica Gomez @mrsjessgomez
Jimmy Casas @casas_jimmy
Latoya Dixon @latoyadixon5
Sanée Bell @SaneeBell
Shelley Burgess @burgess_shelley
Weston Kieschnick @Wes_Kieschnick
Zaretta Hammond @Ready4rigor

ORGANIZATIONS

Association for Supervision and Curriculum
Development (ASCD)
Learning Forward
National Association of Elementary School
Principals (NAESP)
National Association of Secondary School
Principals (NASSP)
Solution Tree

REFERENCES

Abrams, Jennifer. *Hard Conversations Unpacked: The Whos, the Whens, and the What-Ifs.* Thousand Oaks, CA: Corwin, 2016.

Bogel, Anne. *Reading People: How Seeing the World Through the Lens of Personality Changes Everything.* Grand Rapids, MI: Baker Books, 2017.

Brown, Judy. *A Leader's Guide to Reflective Practice.* Bloomington, IN: Trafford Publishing, 2007.

Browne, Joy. *Getting Unstuck: 8 Simple Steps to Solving Any Problem.* New York: Hay House, 2003.

Burgess, Shelley, and Beth Houf. *Lead Like a PIRATE: Make School Amazing for Your Students and Staff.* San Diego, CA: Dave Burgess Consulting, Inc., 2017.

Cabeen, Jessica. *Lead with Grace: Leaning into the Soft Skills of Leadership.* Highland Heights, OH: Times 10 Publications, 2019.

Casas, Jimmy. *Culturize: Every Student. Every Day. Whatever it Takes.* San Diego, CA: Dave Burgess Consulting, Inc., 2017.

Chapman, Gary. *The 5 Love Languages: The Secret to Love That Lasts.* Chicago: Northfield Publishing, 1992.

Curry, Brad, Billy Krakower, and Scott Rocco. *140 Twitter Tips for Educators: Get Connected, Grow Your Professional Learning Network, and Reinvigorate Your Career.* San Diego, CA: Dave Burgess Consulting, Inc., 2016.

Darling-Hammond, Linda. *A License to Teach: Building a Profession for 21s- Century Schools.* New York, NY: Routledge, 2019.

Duckworth, Angela. *Grit: The Power of Passion and Perseverance.* New York: Scribner, 2016.

DuFour, Richard, and Robert J. Marzano. *Leaders of Learning: How District, School, and Classroom Leaders Improve Student Achievement.* Bloomington, IN: Solution Tree, 2011.

DuFour, Richard, Rebecca DuFour, Robert Eaker, Thomas W. Many, and Mike Mattos. *Learning by Doing: A Handbook for Professional Learning Communities at Work.* Bloomington, IN: Solution Tree Press, 2016.

Dweck, Carol S. *Mindset: The New Psychology of Success, How We can Learn to Fulfill Our Potential.* New York: Ballantine Books, 2006.

Elrod, Hal. *The Miracle Morning: The 6 Habits That Will Transform Your Life before 8 a.m.* London: John Murray Learning, 2016.

Hammond, Zaretta. *Culturally Responsive Teaching and the Brain: Promoting Authentic Engagement and Rigor among Culturally and Linguistically Diverse Students.* Thousand Oaks, CA: Corwin, 2015.

Hattie, John. *Visible Learning for Teachers: Maximizing Impact on Learning.* New York: Routledge, 2012.

Navarro, Joe, and Marvin Karlins. *What Every BODY Is Saying: An Ex-FBI Agent's Guide to Speed-Reading People.* New York: HarperCollins, 2008.

Patterson, Kerry, Joseph Grenny, David Maxfield, Ron McMillan, and Al Switzler. *Crucial Accountability: Tools for Resolving Violated Expectations, Broken Commitments, and Bad Behavior,* 2nd ed. New York: McGraw-Hill Education, 2013.

Rath, Tom, and Barry Conchie. *Strengths Based Leadership: Great Leaders, Teams, and Why People Follow.* New York: Gallup Press, 2008.

Reeves, Douglas. *Leading Change in Your School: How to Conquer Myths, Build Commitment, and Get Results.* Alexandria, VA: ASCD, 2009.

Reeves, Douglas. *From Leading to Succeeding: The Seven Elements of Effective Leadership in Education.* Bloomington, IN: Solution Tree, 2016.

Scott, Susan. *Fierce Conversations: Achieving Success at Work and in Life, One Conversation at a Time.* New York: Viking, 2002.

Schmoker, Mike. *Leading with Focus: Elevating the Essentials for School and District Improvement.* Alexandria, VA: ASCD, 2016.

Stone, Douglas, and Sheila Henn. *Thanks for the Feedback: The Science and Art of Receiving Feedback Well.* New York: Penguin Books, 2014.

Van Marter Souers, Kristin and Pete Hall. *Relationship, Responsibility and Regulation: Trauma-Invested Practices for Fostering Resilient Learners.* Alexandria, VA: ASCD, 2019.

Will, Madeline. "5 Things to Know About Today's Teaching Force." *Teacher Beat* (blog). *Education Week*, October 23, 2018. http://blogs.edweek.org/edweek/teacherbeat/2018/10/today_teaching_force_richard_ingersoll.html

ACKNOWLEDGMENTS

It is with deep appreciation that we recognize the impact of those who have launched us personally and professionally, from our incredible mentors who have been there on our brightest and darkest days, to our professional network, which has stretched our imaginations, to our dear families who cleared the path, kept us anchored, and reminded us to be balanced. To our colleagues at the Coalition of Oregon School Administrators (COSA), we would not have connected without the opportunities you provide. We would also like to thank the DBC family for providing us the opportunity to amplify our message through the publishing of this book. Thank you Dave, Shelly, Tara, Marisol, and Lindsey for believing in us and guiding us through the process. We also dedicate this book to the thousands of students, teachers, and school staff who have taught us how important it is to have high expectations, to love unconditionally, and to remember to always keep growing. We are humbly grateful to each of you for supporting us through this project and beyond.

ABOUT THE AUTHORS

KATE BARKER

When someone asks Kate Barker how many children she has, she replies, "Five hundred thirty-seven, plus two." As well as having two children of her own, Kate is currently the principal of Cherry Park Elementary in Portland, Oregon. She has been an educator for the past thirty years, all in the David Douglas School District, which is located in an urban setting. Kate has spent her career dedicated to supporting and learning from her community. She has been a fourth- and fifth-grade teacher and a district office language arts and federal grants leader. In the past seventeen years, she has lovingly served as a principal at three different buildings. In her current building, she works with a diverse and vibrant community of preschool through fifth-grade students. Seventy-five percent of the families experience poverty, and twenty-eight different languages are spoken. Many of her students, whose basic needs are not met, are steeped in trauma. And yet, Cherry Park Elementary students consistently outperform state averages. She holds a master's in special education and is a champion for building a culture that includes *all* students and families. She believes that everything starts with a genuine relationship, and connections and high expectations are at the core of her community's success.

KOURTNEY FERRUA

Social justice has always been central to Kourtney's passion for education, as she began as a teacher's assistant at San Quentin State Prison in 1997. This experience evoked a lifelong dedication to strong educational experiences for all students, especially those who experience the obstacles of inequity. "The relentless belief in every child's unlimited capacity to learn" are words that guide the work she does in McMinnville School District, where she served as principal at Wascher Elementary School for six years and now serves as director of curriculum, instruction, and assessment at the district office. Wascher Elementary was recognized as a Model School by the International Center for Leadership in Education (ICLE) for rapidly improving student outcomes in 2018. In 2019, Kourtney was awarded Oregon's Elementary Principal of the Year and was honored as a National Distinguished Principal. Before entering into administration, Kourtney was a kindergarten and third-grade teacher, as well as an instructional coach. She lives in Oregon's wine country with her husband and two children. Kourtney is on Twitter @kourtneyferrua.

RACHAEL GEORGE

Rachael went from fighting wildland fires with the US Forest Service to putting out fires in the classroom. Education was the last place she thought she'd end up. It wasn't until a hard conversation with a base manager in Grangeville, Idaho, that Rachael realized she needed to put her chainsaw down and make a bigger impact on the world. Rachael is a member of the ASCD Emerging Leaders Class of 2015, and currently serves as the principal of Sandy Grade School in the Oregon Trail School District, located at the base of Mount Hood. Over the past six years, Sandy Grade School has moved from being one of the lowest-ranked elementary schools in the state of Oregon to performing in the top 20 percent of elementary schools. Sandy Grade School has been recognized by the International Center for Leadership in Education (ICLE) as a Model School for closing the achievement gap. Prior to serving as an elementary principal, she was a middle school principal of an "outstanding" and two-time Level 5 Model School, as recognized by the State of Oregon. Rachael specializes in curriculum development, instructional improvement, and working with at-risk students and closing the achievement gap. Connect with Rachael on Twitter @DrRachaelGeorge.

Professional Development and Topics for Speaking Opportunities

KATE:

- Principaled: Navigating the Leadership Learning Curve
- New Principal Academy: Series on How to Survive Being a New Principal
- How to Set Up Social and Behavior Supports So Everyone Is Successful
- Multitiered Systems and Structures for Academics and Behavior
- Effective Data Team Meetings: I Have the Data, Now What?
- Knowing Your People and Navigating Personalities
- The Power of Preschool: You Have a Preschool, Now What?
- Supporting Inclusion in a General Education Setting
- Trauma-Informed Practices: Taking Care of Yourself so You Can Take Care of Your Students

KOURTNEY:

- Principaled: Navigating the Leadership Learning Curve
- Rigor & Joy: Turning Around a Diverse, High-Poverty School by Focusing on High-Leverage Strategies and Embracing Rigor and Joy.
- Powerful Coaching: Leveraging Instructional Leadership through Peer Observations and Clarity

- Mindset Matters: Leveraging Growth Mindset for Student Success

RACHAEL:

- Principaled: Navigating the Leadership Learning Curve
- Your First 100 Days: What You Need to Know When You Land Your First Principal Job
- Academics, Attitude, and Attendance: How to Develop a Culture of Growing All Kids
- Keeping Classrooms Safe, Calm, and Learning: Strategies to Integrate Social-Emotional Learning
- Trauma-Informed Schools: Strategies for Schools and Classrooms to Support the Whole Child
- Math that Works: Using Reteach and Enrich to Excel Math Learning for Students
- The Trials, Tribulations, and Successes of Proficiency-Based Learning

MORE FROM

Since 2012, DBCI has been publishing books that inspire and equip educators to be their best. For more information on our titles or to purchase bulk orders for your school, district, or book study, visit DaveBurgessconsulting.com/DBCIbooks.

Like a PIRATE™ Series

Teach Like a PIRATE by Dave Burgess

eXPlore Like a Pirate by Michael Matera

Learn Like a Pirate by Paul Solarz

Play Like a Pirate by Quinn Rollins

Run Like a Pirate by Adam Welcome

Tech Like a PIRATE by Matt Miller

Lead Like a PIRATE™ Series

Lead Like a PIRATE by Shelley Burgess and Beth Houf

Balance Like a Pirate by Jessica Cabeen, Jessica Johnson, and Sarah Johnson

Lead beyond Your Title by Nili Bartley

Lead with Appreciation by Amber Teamann and Melinda Miller

Lead with Culture by Jay Billy

Lead with Instructional Rounds by Vicki Wilson

Lead with Literacy by Mandy Ellis

Leadership & School Culture

Culturize by Jimmy Casas

Escaping the School Leader's Dunk Tank by Rebecca Coda and Rick Jetter

Fight Song by Kim Bearden

From Teacher to Leader by Starr Sackstein

If the Dance Floor Is Empty, Change the Song by Joe Clark

The Innovator's Mindset by George Couros

It's OK to Say "They" by Christy Whittlesey

Kids Deserve It! by Todd Nesloney and Adam Welcome

Let Them Speak by Rebecca Coda and Rick Jetter

The Limitless School by Abe Hege and Adam Dovico

Live Your Excellence by Jimmy Casas

Next-Level Teaching by Jonathan Alsheimer

The Pepper Effect by Sean Gaillard

The Principled Principal by Jeffrey Zoul and Anthony McConnell

Relentless by Hamish Brewer

The Secret Solution by Todd Whitaker, Sam Miller, and Ryan Donlan

Start. Right. Now. by Todd Whitaker, Jeffrey Zoul, and Jimmy Casas

Stop. Right. Now. by Jimmy Casas and Jeffrey Zoul

Teachers Deserve It by Rae Hughart and Adam Welcome

Teach Your Class Off by CJ Reynolds

They Call Me "Mr. De" by Frank DeAngelis

Thrive through the Five by Jill M. Siler

Unmapped Potential by Julie Hasson and Missy Lennard

When Kids Lead by Todd Nesloney and Adam Dovico

Word Shift by Joy Kirr

Your School Rocks by Ryan McLane and Eric Lowe

Technology & Tools

50 Things You Can Do with Google Classroom by Alice Keeler and Libbi Miller

50 Things to Go Further with Google Classroom by Alice Keeler and Libbi Miller

140 Twitter Tips for Educators by Brad Currie, Billy Krakower, and Scott Rocco

Block Breaker by Brian Aspinall

Code Breaker by Brian Aspinall

Control Alt Achieve by Eric Curts

Google Apps for Littles by Christine Pinto and Alice Keeler

Master the Media by Julie Smith

Reality Bytes by Christine Lion-Bailey, Jesse Lubinsky, and
   Micah Shippee, PhD

Sail the 7 Cs with Microsoft Education by Becky Keene and
   Kathi Kersznowski

Shake Up Learning by Kasey Bell

Social LEADia by Jennifer Casa-Todd

Stepping Up to Google Classroom by Alice Keeler and
   Kimberly Mattina

Teaching Math with Google Apps by Alice Keeler and
   Diana Herrington

Teachingland by Amanda Fox and Mary Ellen Weeks

Teaching Methods & Materials

All 4s and 5s by Andrew Sharos

Boredom Busters by Katie Powell

The Classroom Chef by John Stevens and Matt Vaudrey

The Collaborative Classroom by Trevor Muir

Copyrighteous by Diana Gill

CREATE by Bethany J. Petty

Ditch That Homework by Matt Miller and Alice Keeler

Ditch That Textbook by Matt Miller

Don't Ditch That Tech by Matt Miller, Nate Ridgway, and
   Angelia Ridgway

EDrenaline Rush by John Meehan

Educated by Design by Michael Cohen, The Tech Rabbi

The EduProtocol Field Guide by Marlena Hebern and Jon Corippo

The EduProtocol Field Guide: Book 2 by Marlena Hebern and
   Jon Corippo

Instant Relevance by Denis Sheeran

LAUNCH by John Spencer and A.J. Juliani

Make Learning MAGICAL by Tisha Richmond

Pure Genius by Don Wettrick

The Revolution by Darren Ellwein and Derek McCoy

Shift This! by Joy Kirr

Skyrocket Your Teacher Coaching by Michael Cary Sonbert

Spark Learning by Ramsey Musallam

Sparks in the Dark by Travis Crowder and Todd Nesloney

Table Talk Math by John Stevens

The Wild Card by Hope and Wade King

The Writing on the Classroom Wall by Steve Wyborney

Inspiration, Professional Growth & Personal Development

Be REAL by Tara Martin

Be the One for Kids by Ryan Sheehy

The Coach ADVenture by Amy Illingworth

Creatively Productive by Lisa Johnson

Educational Eye Exam by Alicia Ray

The EduNinja Mindset by Jennifer Burdis

Empower Our Girls by Lynmara Colón and Adam Welcome

Finding Lifelines by Andrew Grieve and Andrew Sharos

The Four O'Clock Faculty by Rich Czyz

How Much Water Do We Have? by Pete and Kris Nunweiler

P Is for Pirate by Dave and Shelley Burgess

A Passion for Kindness by Tamara Letter

The Path to Serendipity by Allyson Apsey

Sanctuaries by Dan Tricarico

The SECRET SAUCE by Rich Czyz

Shattering the Perfect Teacher Myth by Aaron Hogan

Stories from Webb by Todd Nesloney

Talk to Me by Kim Bearden

Teach Better by Chad Ostrowski, Tiffany Ott, Rae Hughart, and Jeff Gargas

Teach Me, Teacher by Jacob Chastain
Teach, Play, Learn! by Adam Peterson
The Teachers of Oz by Herbie Raad and Nathan Lang-Raad
TeamMakers by Laura Robb and Evan Robb
Through the Lens of Serendipity by Allyson Apsey
The Zen Teacher by Dan Tricarico

Children's Books

Beyond Us by Aaron Polansky
Cannonball In by Tara Martin
Dolphins in Trees by Aaron Polansky
I Want to Be a Lot by Ashley Savage
The Princes of Serendip by Allyson Apsey
The Wild Card Kids by Hope and Wade King
Zom-Be a Design Thinker by Amanda Fox